FROM SAVAGES TO SUBJECTS

Latin American Realities

Robert M. Levine, Series Editor

AFRO-BRAZILIAN CULTURE AND POLITICS
Bahia, 1790s–1990s
Hendrik Kraay, Editor

BITITA'S DIARY
Childhood Memoirs of Carolina Maria de Jesus
Carolina Maria de Jesus, Author
Robert M. Levine, Editor
Emanuelle Oliveira and Beth Joan Vinkler, Translators

FIGHTING SLAVERY IN THE CARIBBEAN
The Life and Times of a British Family in Nineteenth-Century Havana
Luis Martínez-Fernández

FROM SAVAGES TO SUBJECTS
Missions in the History of the American Southwest
Robert H. Jackson

MAYA REVOLT AND REVOLUTION IN THE 18TH CENTURY
Robert W. Patch

PILLAGING THE EMPIRE
Piracy in the Americas, 1500–1750
Kris E. Lane

POLITICS AND EDUCATION IN ARGENTINA, 1946–1962
Mónica Esti Rein
Martha Grenzeback, Translator

THE SWEAT OF THEIR BROW
A History of Work in Latin America
David J. McCreery

THE SWORD OF HUNGER
A Latin American History
Roberta Delson and Robert M. Levine
(forthcoming)

FROM SAVAGES TO SUBJECTS

MISSIONS IN THE HISTORY OF THE AMERICAN SOUTHWEST

ROBERT H. JACKSON

Taylor & Francis Group
LONDON AND NEW YORK

First published 2000 by M.E. Sharpe, Inc.

Published 2017 by Routledge
2 Park Square, Milton Park, Abingdon, Oxon OX14 4RN
711 Third Avenue, New York, NY 10017, USA

Routledge is an imprint of the Taylor & Francis Group, an informa business

Copyright © 2000 by Taylor & Francis

No part of this book may be reprinted or reproduced or utilised in any form or by any electronic, mechanical, or other means, now known or hereafter invented, including photocopying and recording, or in any information storage or retrieval system, without permission in writing from the publishers.

Notices

No responsibility is assumed by the publisher for any injury and/or damage to persons or property as a matter of products liability, negligence or otherwise, or from any use of operation of any methods, products, instructions or ideas contained in the material herein.

Practitioners and researchers must always rely on their own experience and knowledge in evaluating and using any information, methods, compounds, or experiments described herein. In using such information or methods they should be mindful of their own safety and the safety of others, including parties for whom they have a professional responsibility.

Product or corporate names may be trademarks or registered trademarks, and are used only for identification and explanation without intent to infringe.

Library of Congress Cataloging-in-Publication Data

Jackson, Robert H.
  From savages to subjects : missions in the history of the American Southwest / Robert H. Jackson.
    p. cm. – (Latin American realities)
  Includes bibliographical references and index.
  ISBN 0–7656–0597–X (hardcover) ISBN 0–7656–0598–8 (pbk)
  1. Indians of North America—Missions—Southwest, New. 2. Indians, Treatment of—Southwest, New. 3. Missions—Southwest, New—History. I. Title. II. Series.

E78.S7 J195 2000
266'.279—dc21   99–087712

ISBN 13: 978-0-7656-0598-6 (pbk)
ISBN 13: 978-0-7656-0597-9 (hbk)

Table of Contents

List of Illustrations	vii
Foreword	ix
Introduction	xi
1. Mission Economics: Production and Labor, Supply, and Local Markets	3
2. The Building of the Missions	28
3. Social and Cultural Change	57
4. Indigenous Resistance and Social Control	68
5. The Demise of the Indian Populations in the Missions	89
6. The Demise of the Mission System	116
7. Conclusions	126
Bibliographic Essay	131
Index	141

Illustrations

Tables

1.1 Selected Commodity Prices in Pesos and Reales, 1745–1772   12
1.2 Prices of Selected Spices in Reales, 1746–1772   13
1.3 Prices in Reales of Selected Goods Shipped to San Diego Mission, 1774–1811   14
1.4 Prices in Reales of Selected Goods Shipped to Santa Clara Mission, 1779–1810   16
1.5 Prices in Reales of Selected Goods Shipped to San José Mission, 1800–1812   17
2.1 Building Construction Reported at Rosario Mission, 1794–1800   44
2.2 Building Construction Reported at Santo Tomás Mission, 1794–1801   46
2.3 Building Construction Reported at La Purísima Mission   48

Figures

1.1 Price of Wine Shipped to San Diego Mission, 1782–1804   21
1.2 Price of Wine Shipped to Santa Clara Mission, 1782–1809   22
2.1 Plan of San Fernando Mission Located in Northern Baja California   41
2.2 Plan of Rosario Mission Located in Northern Baja California   43
2.3 Plan of Santa Catalina Mission Located in Northern Baja California   45
2.4 View (c. 1880) of the ruins of the first site of La Purísima Mission, showing the configuration of the main building complex   47

2.5	Diagram (c. 1818) Showing a Section of the Building Complex of Santa Clara Mission	49
2.6	Photograph (c. 1880) of the Ruins of the First Site of La Purísima Mission, Lompoc, California	51
2.7	Ruins of the First Site of La Purísima Mission, Lompoc, California	52
2.8	Reconstructed Buildings at the Second Site of La Purísima Mission, Lompoc, California	54
5.1	Population of Rosario Mission, 1754–1806	97
5.2	Baptisms of Converts and Births Recorded at San Antonio Mission, 1771–1840	101
5.3	Burials Recorded at San Antonio Mission, 1771–1840	102
5.4	Indigenous Population of New Mexico, 1598–1821	103
5.5	Population of Tumacacori Mission, 1761–1820	106
5.6	Population of the California Missions, 1790–1842	109
6.1	Cattle, Sheep, and Horses Reported at Thirteen California Missions, 1830–1839	121
6.2	Value of Selected California Mission Estates, 1834/35 and 1845	123

Maps

2.1	Nuevo México	30
2.2	Sonora	32
2.3	Texas and Northern Mexico	34
2.4a	Baja California, North	36
2.4b	Baja California, South	37
2.5	Alta California	38

Foreword

The "Latin American Realities" series presents aspects of life not usually covered in standard histories that tell the stories of governments, economic development, and institutions. Books in this series dwell on different facets of life, equally important, but not often analyzed or described. How have underground economies worked? What strategies have poor people employed to cope with hardship and to improve their lives? How have government policies impacted everyday life? What has been the importance of popular culture? How have members of minority or disadvantaged peoples in Latin America—blacks, recent immigrants, indigenous peoples, men and women of intermediate racial status—fared? How have social and economic changes affected them?

Some of us forget that present-day California, during the seventeenth and eighteenth centuries, was northern Mexico. Professor Robert H. Jackson, in his thoroughly researched and provocative study of this region, avoids the usual focus on, in his words, the "heroic missionaries and steadfast soldiers." Rather, he examines the lives of the indigenous peoples who were brought to live in the missions, where they would learn to obey the Spanish king, become converted to Christianity, and be taught that Spanish culture elevated the soul while their own heritage degraded it.

The northern reaches of the Spanish New World Empire included not only California but New Mexico, Arizona, Colorado, Nevada, and Texas. *From Savages to Subjects: Missions in the History of the American Southwest* explores a broad array of themes, from the underlying colonial economic goals that led to forced Indian labor to the building of the missions to the social and cultural trauma of pacification to the ultimate demise of the Indian mission population. The Spaniards dealt brutally with any evidence of the survival of Indian beliefs or with what they considered to be laziness. Women suspected of aborting their fetuses or killing their infants were lashed for nine days in succession (the punishment was called a *novena*) and made to stand in public outside of church in leg irons holding a wooden doll to symbolize the lost child.

Professor Jackson explains how the Spanish government failed to reach its goal of achieving stable indigenous communities except in New Mexico, where the population had traditionally lived in sedentary villages. Some Indians reached accommodation with their overseers, while others resisted. The legacy of this experience, as the author concludes, has lasted down through the present day.

Robert M. Levine

Introduction

The mission system that developed in the northernmost reaches of colonial Mexico in the seventeenth and eighteenth centuries has been the subject of considerable scholarship, as well as scholarly and popular controversy. For years most studies of the missions were what can be characterized as triumphal church self-history that at times tended toward hagiography. Controversy has surrounded sticky questions such as the consequences of the mission system for native peoples and campaigns to glorify the work of the missionaries. The glorification of the missionaries has gone to the extremes. There is in California documentation of a well-organized and -funded campaign to declare Father Junipero Serra, O.F.M., a saint. Serra was the architect of the California mission system. The Serra canonization campaign resurrected emotions surrounding what some view as the mistreatment of the indigenous population at the hands of the Franciscan missionaries. Moreover, in justifying canonization, academics who support the Serra cause emphasized the civilizing of savages.

The triumphalism of the Catholic Church self-history emphasizes the positive influence of the missionaries on the indigenous populations and the sacredness of the missionaries' venture. However, the history of the frontier missions in northern Mexico is far more complex than the older image of pious missionaries sacrificing their lives to save the souls of savage natives suggests. It is the history of a well-designed system aimed at achieving very specific policy goals and the ways that native peoples responded to the mission program. The Spanish colonial system evolved in central Mexico on the basis of the exploitation of sedentary indigenous populations living in corporate communities. The Spanish created a system of indirect rule that made indigenous leaders responsible for collecting tribute (a head tax) and rounding up workers to serve on drafts that provided Spanish entrepreneurs with cheap labor. The Spanish government financed missions in order to transform the native peoples living on the northern Mexican frontier into a sedentary population that would fit into the existing system that already functioned in the south.

Through a series of papal concessions called the *real patronato* (royal patronage), the Spanish government exercised a great deal of control over the Catholic Church, which was the institution that also gave the Spanish a rationale for conquest and exploitation. The government saw itself as the defender of the only true faith and assumed responsibility for evangelization of the indigenous populations in the New World. Moreover, the Catholic Church served as a bulwark for the colonial order, and indoctrinated the *plebe* (commoners) to obey the colonial order. In many ways the church was an arm of the government and worked in conjunction with the government to solidify the new social order in Mexico.

The native peoples of northern Mexico did not live in sophisticated stratified and hierarchical state systems, although in some areas such as Sonora and New Mexico the population was sedentary and lived in village or tribal states. Some groups were sedentary farmers, whereas in other areas, such as Baja California and parts of Texas, the natives were nomadic hunters and gatherers. None of these native peoples were deemed to be sufficiently advanced to be included in colonial society as autonomous corporate indigenous communities. The Spanish thus intended to christianize and civilize the indigenous population and prepare them to serve a preset role in the new colonial system.

The missionary evangelization campaign in central Mexico was in many ways the precursor to the missions on the northern frontier of Mexico. In the half-century following the conquest of the Mexica Aztec tribute state, members of different missionary orders such as the Franciscans, Dominicans, Augustinians, and Mercederians divided up the sedentary populations of central Mexico into spheres of influence. They created feudal-like fiefs that their native charges at times defended in bloody assaults on rival mission fiefs. By mid-century the missionaries had completed campaigns of mass conversion and directed the construction of massive fortress monasteries. Even as the missionary orders consolidated their control over the native population, the secular clergy complained to the Crown that the missionaries had accomplished their goal of conversion and should now give way to administration by the secular clergy. The Crown resolved the dispute in the mid-1570s in favor of the secular clergy and ordered the missionary orders to give up their village fiefs and move on to the evangelization of indigenous groups on the frontier.

There were several other legacies from the early missionary experience in central Mexico that would prove to be important in the frontier missions. Missionaries were given a degree of control over the Indians living on the missions, both spiritual and temporal. The missionary assumed the role of the paternalistic father to natives legally defined as children (*niños con barbas,* or children with beards) and by law were permitted to use corporal punishment to discipline them. This continued to be an important aspect of the mission program on the frontier missions. The second legacy was a ten-year legal limit placed on the term that the missionaries could administer indigenous communities, a legal limit that proved to be impractical in northern Mexico. However, this law was a direct response to the behavior of the missionary orders in central Mexico and the pattern of institutional complacency among the missionary orders once the mass conversion of the native population had been largely accomplished.

The missionaries stationed on the northern frontier enjoyed control over all aspects of the lives of the indigenous converts living at the missions, as had their predecessors in central Mexico in the decades immediately following the Spanish conquest. This included management of the mission economies and the use of indigenous labor in different economic activities. In some instances the missionaries assigned heads of household plots of land that they worked on their own account, but all adults were assigned to work on communal projects. These included farming, tending herds of livestock, craft production, and building construction. Indian workers constructed the fortress monasteries of central Mexico and built the extensive building complexes on the frontier missions. When native workers did not fulfill their assigned duties, or in other ways violated the strict rules imposed by the missionaries, they received exemplary punishment.

In the second half of the sixteenth century the Spanish government faced its first serious challenge on the near northern frontier (the frontier just north of newly conquered New Spain) during a protracted conflict known as the Chichimec War (1550–1590). The discovery of silver deposits at Zacatecas set off a mining boom, and the Spanish frontier rapidly advanced to the north before the pacification of nomadic bands of hunter-gatherers collectively known as the Chichimecs (a derogatory Nahuatl term). The miners in Zacatecas relied on supplies shipped from

Mexico City or Guadalajara, and the large supply trains became easy targets for raids by the Chichimec bands. For forty years the Spanish attempted a military solution to the Chichimec raids but faced constant frustration from highly mobile bands that adopted the use of the horse and restructured their society around raiding the Spanish. Eventually the Spanish abandoned warfare in favor of a new approach. The government offered Chichimec bands incentives to settle in permanent villages managed by missionaries. The missionaries worked to transform the society, culture, religion, and worldview of the natives. Moreover, the government settled small colonies of sedentary natives from central Mexico in the new communities to serve as role models for the newly settled Chichimecs. The new policy accelerated the pacification of the Chichimecs, and served as a model for the missions established further north, including the settlement of more acculturated indigenous converts at the missions.

The settlement of more acculturated converts functioned in two ways. In some instances the government sent colonies of indigenous peoples from central Mexico. For example, the settlement of Saltillo in southern Coahuila included the establishment of a colony of Tlaxcaltecos from the province of Tlaxcala just east of Mexico City. In the Pimería Alta region of northern Sonora, on the other hand, Jesuit missionaries brought Opata converts from central Sonora to help manage the new mission communities and to serve as role models. Yaquis from southern Sonora also migrated to the northern frontier in the province, and some worked in the missions as well.

Three orders established and managed missions on the northern frontier of Mexico. The two most important were the Franciscans and, until their expulsion by the Spanish empire in 1768, the Jesuits. The Franciscans, or Grey Robes, were the first missionaries to work in Mexico. The first twelve arrived in 1524, and were the most important of the missionary orders in central Mexico. The Franciscans established the missions in New Mexico, Coahuila, and Texas, and after 1769 Alta California. Initially the Grey Robes organized themselves into provinces, and the different provinces supplied and staffed the missions. In the late seventeenth century the Franciscans reorganized their missionary enterprise along lines established by the *propaganda fide* in Rome. The propaganda fide was a bureaucracy organized to better promote Catholic evangelization efforts throughout the world, particularly outside of Europe. In Mexico the Franciscans established apostolic colleges in Queretaro, Zacatecas, and later Mexico City. The colleges trained the

Franciscans for service in the frontier missions and also managed groups of missions for the government.

The Jesuits (Society of Jesus, or Black Robes) were the most capable missionaries and were also an international organization with members from throughout Europe and European colonial possessions including Spanish America. The international composition of the Society of Jesus caused some concern for the Spanish government, which ultimately favored the Franciscans following the expulsion of the Jesuits. The Franciscans stationed in Mexico came only from Spanish territory. Jesuits initially arrived in Mexico to establish educational institutions for colonial elites, but then established frontier missions in Sinaloa, Sonora, Nueva Vizcaya (Durango and Chihuahua), and Baja California. They also attempted to establish missions in Florida, but with little success. The expulsion of the Jesuits in 1768 created considerable staffing difficulty for the Franciscans assigned to replace them.

Baja California was one of the mission groupings that the Franciscans staffed following the Jesuit expulsion. The peninsula missions were unique, because the Jesuits themselves had funded the establishments following failed government-financed colonization schemes. The Jesuits established an endowment to fund the missions and founded new missions only when they had funds for an endowment. The Jesuits had also exercised complete administrative control over the peninsula colony, including control over the military. The Franciscans from the apostolic college of San Fernando (Mexico City) staffed the Baja California missions for only a few years (1768–1773) and used the peninsula as a base from which to colonize Alta California. However, the Dominicans applied for ex-Jesuit missions, and reached an agreement with the Franciscans to assume administrative responsibilities for the peninsula missions along with a large district along the Pacific Coast that would serve as a field for the extension of evangelization through the establishment of new missions. The Dominicans administered Baja California until the 1820s and 1830s and limited their work on the frontier to Baja California.

This book explores the development of the missions in northern Mexico, focusing on those regions that now form part of the United States (New Mexico, Arizona, Texas, and the Californias). It is not a history of heroic missionaries and steadfast soldiers and colonial administrators. Rather, it examines the experience of the natives brought to live on the missions and the ways in which the mission program attempted to change just about all aspects of indigenous life. In this volume, there are five thematic chapters that contain different information on the missions in the regions examined here. It should be pointed out that the amount of information available differs from region to region. Many documents simply have not survived.

Chapter 1 explores the development of mission economics, the use of native labor, and the relationship between the missions and local and regional markets. Nonindigenous settlement and economic activities around mining, farming, and ranching dictated the development or lack of development of market-style economies. Sonora was the only region considered here that developed a market economy, although trade did occur between New Mexico and Texas and the provinces further south. Missionaries sold surplus communal production and in some cases supplied the military garrisons. The Franciscans stationed in Alta California, on the other hand, reached a formal agreement with the government in Mexico City to supply most of the needs of the military garrisons. This agreement profoundly changed the development of all California missions.

Social, cultural, and religious change was at the core of the mission program and is considered in chapter 2. The coverage is uneven because of available sources, but this chapter does provide examples of the ways in which the missionaries attempted to change virtually every aspect of the lives of the Indians. This change also included the way in which the natives worked and their conditioning to accept a new role in colonial society as laborers and tribute payers. This aspect of the mission program is considered in chapter 1; chapter 2 focuses on such issues as religious conversion and change in material culture.

The native peoples living on both sides of the Spanish-Indian frontier resisted Spanish colonial domination. The authors of Church self-history viewed resistance as the work of the devil and as part of the fickle nature of the native population. Their view generally reflects the view of the missionaries, who saw themselves as stern fathers correcting their naughty children when they resisted paternalistic control and authority. Motives for resistance were complex and are the subject of chapter 3. Considered here is resistance among Indians congregated on the missions, as well as raids on Spanish settlements by indigenous groups living beyond the pale of Spanish control. The missionaries responded to resistance with measures of social control. One concern that the missionaries had, for example, was that the Indians were promiscuous and did not respect family values. In some missions the missionaries incarcerated single women and girls at night in unhealthful dormitories.

In most of the regions examined here, the mission system ultimately did not accomplish its goal of creating a stable sedentary population of indigenous subjects of the Crown. One reason was demographic collapse of the indigenous populations all across the northern frontier of Mexico. Chapter 4 outlines the causes and manifestations of demographic collapse, including epidemic and endemic disease and in some instances policies of social control that exacerbated problems of public health.

In the late eighteenth and early nineteenth centuries, reform-minded royal officials and Spanish and Mexican liberal politicians criticized the paternalism of the missions, which they believed prevented the full integration of the indigenous population into Mexican society and political life. They advocated the closing of the missions and the emancipation of the natives, who would now assume their proper place in frontier society. Moreover, some liberals also attacked Church wealth, which they believed also retarded Mexican economic development. The demise of the indigenous population was one justification given for closing the missions, yet at the same time some missionaries argued against closing the missions, pointing out that they continued to congregate and evangelize. Chapter 5 outlines the demise of the missions and the disposition of the land, buildings, livestock, and equipment making up the mission estates—all of which, at least theoretically, were to be distributed among the surviving natives. The Indians did not always receive the fruits of their labor.

By way of conclusion I draw comparisons among the missions studied in this book. This discussion again summarizes the major themes developed in Chapters 1 to 5, and offers some parting thoughts on what the mission experience meant.

FROM SAVAGES TO SUBJECTS

Chapter 1

Mission Economics
Production and Labor, Supply, and Local Markets

Economic production and provision were important aspects of the frontier mission project. Economic development entailed either the harnessing of existing production for the needs of the missionaries, civil/military officials, and settlers, or the organization of an entirely new economic system that often had to introduce European notions of disciplined labor. The full range of mission economies evolved on the frontier of northern New Spain. In New Mexico and Sonora, for example, the missionaries erected mission communities in functioning indigenous communities with well-developed economies based upon agriculture, skilled artisan production and trade, and some hunting and collection of wild plant foods. At the other extreme were the missions of Texas (excluding the missions built among the Hasinais) and the Californias. The indigenous populations of these regions were largely semi-sedentary hunters and gatherers who exploited food resources in a clearly defined territory and frequently practiced a pattern of seasonal transhumance between village sites occupied over a long period of time.

The discussion of patterns of mission economic development in this chapter focuses on three areas: production and labor, the supply of goods not found locally to the missions, and the relationship between the missions and local/regional markets. This chapter also makes distinctions between economic patterns on the missions established among sedentary peoples (New Mexico, northern Sonora), and among semisedentary/nomadic hunters and gatherers (California and Texas). The first topic is production and the organization of labor on the missions.

Production and Labor

The primary objective of the missionaries was to provide basic sustenance for the Indians congregated on the missions and for themselves and to see that any surpluses be sold locally to earn extra money for the mission beyond the funds allocated by the government for each establishment. The Franciscans in New Mexico created missions at existing indigenous communities with well-established economies based upon agriculture, specialized craft production, and trade. The missionaries could organize labor drafts for construction projects such as fortress churches and *conventos* (convents). The large size of the Pueblo populations in the seventeenth century allowed the Franciscans to initiate major construction projects, such as the stone churches built on the Salinas missions (Humanas, Abo, Quarai) and Pecos. Additionally, the Franciscans controlled lands specifically set aside for their support and for that of the mission program. They used the crops and livestock from these lands for their own support, but also sold surpluses for profit.

A central goal in the missions was social-cultural engineering. The Franciscans stationed in New Mexico operated schools designed to teach the natives new skills such as mechanical arts and new weaving techniques. The Franciscans sold mission-produced products locally and in neighboring regions such as Chihuahua. There was some trade in the seventeenth and early eighteenth centuries, but at the end of the eighteenth century the demand for New Mexico textiles and pottery in Chihuahua grew, creating new sources of revenue for the missionaries. The missionaries also introduced new crops and improved agricultural techniques.

In the seventeenth century, Spanish settlers also exploited Indian labor through the *encomienda* system. The encomienda first evolved as a feudal institution in southern Spain beginning in the thirteenth century, and the conquistadors first introduced the institution to Caribbean and then to the mainland in the sixteenth century. The encomienda generally was a grant of jurisdiction over a specific group of Indian heads of household, and it entitled the holder of the grant to collect tribute, labor, and personal services. Juan de Oñate introduced the encomienda to New Mexico around 1600, and distributed grants to Pueblo Indians and sections of Pueblos to his followers. Later in the century the number of grants was fixed at thirty-five. Typically, the Indians paid tribute in units of corn, animal skins (buffalo and deer), and cotton *mantas* (cloths). In the 1660s, for example, tribute collected was measured in units based on the numbers of heads of household. Pecos had the largest tribute with 340 units as compared to 110 for Taos, 80 for half of Shonopovi, 50 for half of Acoma, and 30 for half of Abo. There was also a labor draft known as *repartimiento* linked to the encomienda that provided workers for farms and large livestock estates. Theoretically workers received a daily wage of half a real (later raised in 1659 to one real), but the Indians commonly did not receive pay. Disputes between missionaries and settlers over encomiendas were common, and excesses and abuses associated with the institution contributed to the 1680 Pueblo revolt. Following the reconquest of New Mexico after 1692 by Diego de Vargas, the encomienda was no longer an important institution. Moreover, the predominance of small farms, usually worked directly by the settlers themselves, limited the demand for Indian labor.

A similar pattern developed in northern Sonora. The northern Pimas continued to control individual parcels of land for family production, while the missionaries managed lands to support the mission operations and expenses not covered by government funds. The stark realities of an arid environment at some sites in Sonora, however, limited the self-sufficiency of some of the mission communities.

The Jesuits who staffed the Pimería Alta missions attempted to assert spiritual and temporal control over the Indians living in the mission communities. This meant that the Jesuits made the decisions regarding exploitation of communal resources from agriculture to the production of cloth and leather goods, as well as the administration of livestock and communal mission property. The Jesuits required adult Indian converts to work on communal projects, and the government authorized the Jesuits and all frontier missionaries to use corporal punishment to ensure discipline and to correct perceived violations of the strict moral codes they wished to impose on the Indians. The Jesuits usually did not administer corporal punishment themselves, but gave responsibility for its direct administration to Indian village officials.

The northern Pimas continued to cultivate their own parcels, and the crops grown on these parcels were not a part of the communal mission produce. In this fashion the missionaries hoped to break down the kin-based social relationships that cemented native society and to stress the nuclear family as the basic unit of social organization. As in New Mexico, the Pimas were closer to making the transition to full *indio* status—that is, they provided labor, paid tribute, and lived in self-governing indigenous villages. However, the missionaries also attempted to eliminate pre-Hispanic communal food collection activities such as the harvesting of cactus fruit or hunting.

Wheat and corn were the most important grains grown at the missions on communal lands, with wheat being first in importance. Only a few figures on grain production survive. Between 1749 and 1762, for example, the crops grown at Aconchi and Baviacora in central Sonora totaled 10,429 *fanegas* (2.6 bushels) of wheat and 3,861 fanegas of corn. The missionaries sold 18 percent of the wheat and 42 percent of the corn grown. Similarly, wheat was the dominant crop grown in the Pimería Alta missions: between 1818 and 1820, wheat production in the region totaled 5,942 fanegas, as against 313 a mere fanegas of corn and 271 fanegas of frijol. The missions also had herds of cattle, sheep and goats, horses, and swine. The missionaries frequently complained about the loss of livestock to raiding Indians such as the Apaches. The Jesuits complained about the loss of livestock. However, grain sales constituted the single largest source of revenue for the Sonora missions. For example, between 1720 and 1766 grain sales by the Jesuits stationed at San Pedro de Aconchi totaled 72,826 pesos as against 9,606 pesos for sales of livestock.

Following the expulsion of the Jesuits in 1767–68 the imperial reformer José de Galvez initiated a new system in the missions. The Franciscans who replaced the Jesuits in the Pimería Alta no longer controlled mission temporalities, and the government appointed civil administrators to manage the mission economies. The Franciscans were simply to function as parish priests to the indios living on the missions. Galvez's experiment amounted to a partial secularization of the missions, but the new regime lasted only until 1769, when Galvez reversed his earlier order and restored the mission temporalities to the control of the Franciscans. From the very beginning the Franciscans complained about the failings of the new system. They attributed the lack of discipline among the Indians to the loss of control over the temporalities, and the fact that the Indians had been told they no longer needed to work for the missionaries. They also pointed out that the civil commissioners appointed to administer the missions dissipated the property such as livestock and allowed the Indians to take stored food.

Debate over the management of the Pimería Alta missions did not end in 1769. In 1772, Tubac presidio commander Juan Bautista de Anza challenged the basic foundation of the missions. He argued that the Indians were required to provide too much labor to the missionaries, and de Anza proposed that the obligatory labor of the Indians should be replaced by a system of voluntary labor. He also stated that the Franciscans should not control the mission temporalities. De Anza also urged the government to establish schools for the Indians and to encourage the indios to have more contact with the settlers living in the region. The government rejected his plan, which would have resulted in greater integration of Indians into frontier society.

In the following year Diego Ximeno, O.F.M., responded to de Anza's proposals with a Franciscan plan eventually endorsed by the government. Ximeno requested that the missionaries be given undisputed control over mission temporalities. The temporalities consisted of the authority to (a) supervise Indian labor and punish the Indians; (b) end labor drafts that took Indian laborers away from the missions; (c) mediate interactions between the Indians and Spaniards, as well as ban settlers' living among the Indians. In granting Ximeno's petition, the government rejected de Anza's proposal to more rapidly integrate the Pimas into frontier society. Instead, the government opted in favor of the existing system of paternalism under the Franciscans, who attempted to shield as much as possible the converts living in the missions from Spanish society, as Franciscan missionaries had attempted to do in Mexico since the sixteenth century. However, the serious questioning of the continued operation of the Pimería Alta missions made it imperative for the Franciscans to justify the continuation of the mission system by documenting the continued congregation and conversion of pagans.

Tinkering with the system continued until the secularization of the missions following Mexican independence, and civil officials and missionaries drafted reports on how to improve the system. One such report in 1814 on Bac mission in the Pimería Alta reflected a changed philosophy among the Franciscans that responded to the changing mood of the government. The installation of a liberal *cortes* (parliament) in Spain that in 1813 called into question the continued functioning of the missions posed a major challenge to the Franciscans. Juan de Cevallos, O.F.M., made recommendations in his report that essentially reversed the stand taken by the Franciscans sixty years earlier. Cevallos urged the hiring of a teacher to educate the Pimas; the distribution of mission lands and water rights to the Indians; adoption of a policy to rent mission lands to settlers; the use of salaried laborers, either Indian or settlers, to work mission lands; and the sale of mission livestock to cover mission expenses. On the other hand, Cevallos embraced the century-old concern of the missionaries for the provision of European-style clothing to the Indians, especially women.

The organization of the economy of the missions in Texas and California was somewhat different from that already examined in New Mexico and the Pimería Alta. The indigenous peoples congregated on the missions were not sedentary agriculturists, which meant that the missionaries had to introduce an entirely different economic organization based on agriculture and ranching. In the case of Baja California, the arid climate limited farming to sites with some water, so in the early stages of mission development most of the Indians did not reside at the central mission village, and rotated in periodically for religious instruction. However, as the indigenous population declined, more and more people came to live at the main settlement. Moreover, the Jesuits also imported food from the Mexican mainland, primarily Sinaloa and Sonora. In the Texas case, particularly in the San Antonio missions, the Franciscans imported wheat from Saltillo, and concentrated on growing corn and other crops.

In all three areas the missionaries enrolled adult men and women in the communal labor force, and exercised control over the mission temporalities. Indian children became adults when they reached age twelve to thirteen, and at that point were incorporated into the labor force. Generally, the heads of household did not receive individual plots of land, and the missions operated large communal kitchens that prepared meals for all of the converts. The missionaries established a far more paternalistic regime in Texas and the California, and imposed rigid social control enforced through different forms of corporal punishment. The evidence shows that the Franciscans in the Alta California establishments imposed stricter social control. In all three areas the teaching of new skills was one aspect of a larger program of drastic social, religious, and cultural change, and the creation of a disciplined labor force was consistent with the larger goal of transforming the indigenous populations in conformity to Spanish policy objectives.

The organization of the economies of the three regions and their labor systems were similar. For purposes of illustrating patterns of economic development, I focus on the example of the Alta California establishments, for which there is abundant documentation. The economy of the Alta California missions was based on agriculture, ranching, and craft industries such as textile production. The Franciscans controlled two important resources: abundant land and Indian labor. The mission domain granted to La Purísima, for example, covered some 84 square leagues, or about 149,000 hectares of land. Within this territory the Franciscans developed farming and ranching at different sites. In the 1830s the mission included seven ranchos dedicated to agriculture and ranching. The 1773 agreement between the Franciscans and the colonial government stipulated that the missions would supply the military with food, textiles, and leather goods. Therefore the missionaries organized the economy of the missions to produce large surpluses, unlike the mission economies of Texas and Baja California largely geared to self-sufficiency. The Franciscans also hired out Indian labor to both the military and local settlers, and large numbers of Indians from the missions worked on building projects, producing crops, tending livestock, and craft production.

The Franciscans supplied food and other goods directly to the *presidios* and the military guard stationed at each mission. The common practice was to hire *mayordomos* (overseers) to be directly responsible for the day-to-day management of the different economic activities at the missions. The Franciscans recruited overseers from either the local settler population, or else from the soldiers. Members of the mission guard often doubled as overseers. Overseers earned a salary in addition to food rations.

Wheat, corn, and barley were the most important crops grown at the missions. Cultural factors played an important role in the decision on the choice of crops grown. Spaniards and settlers in northern Mexico perceived corn to be an inferior "Indian" grain, and preferred wheat. Even today, the population of northern Mexico consumes wheat tortillas, whereas the population of central Mexico eats corn tortillas. However, corn produced more grain per unit planted than wheat. At La Purísima, for example, the ratio of wheat harvested to planted ranged between 2 to 24 fanegas (2.6 bushels), but corn ranged from a low of 1 to 333 fanegas, and was consistently higher than wheat. Production levels fluctuated from year to year, but the largest wheat harvest was 4,000 fanegas in 1821 and that of corn 2,000 fanegas in 1813 and 1814.

In most years La Purísima produced more wheat than corn and barley combined. The Franciscans emphasized wheat over corn despite the greater productivity of corn and the large Indian population at the mission that primarily ate corn. The obligation to supply the military prompted the decision to grow more wheat than corn. Moreover, the

Franciscans supplied the needs of the military without regard to actual production levels. In other words, the missionaries provided less food to the Indians following poor harvests in order to supply the military.

The missions also owned large herds of cattle, sheep, and horses. Slaughtered livestock provided protein for the diet of the Indians, and also leather and wool for producing clothing, shoes, and other items consumed by the Indians, soldiers, and settlers. After about 1800, an increasing number of foreign ships visited the California coast, bringing in particular Americans, who developed trade with the missions and, to a lesser extent, settlers. After 1820 the scale of trade grew, and the Franciscans sold large numbers of cattle hides and tallow (rendered fat). The annual reports indicate the overculling of cattle herds to produce hides and tallow for export at some missions after 1800. There is some evidence of overculling at a number of missions including La Purísima. In 1809, the missionaries reported 10,000 cattle, but this number rapidly dropped over the next several years to a low of 4,000 in 1812. The numbers slowly grew and reached 11,000 in 1821. However, there were several significant one-year drops in the 1820s. For example, from 1824 to 1825 the number of cattle reported declined from 10,500 to 6,000. This may represent a weakness in the count of the number of animals, perhaps related to the 1824 Chumash uprising.

A second important aspect of the mission economies was the supply of goods from central Mexico. An analysis of the mission supply system provides important insights into the workings and limitations of mission production. Moreover, the list of goods imported to the frontier missions provides clues about the internal social structure and the status of different individuals. The missionaries in all of the regions studied here imported goods from central Mexico. The discussion here focuses on a case study of the supply of the Texas and Alta California missions.

The Supply of the Missions

The primary economic objective of the Franciscans stationed in the Texas missions was to produce enough food to feed the Indians congregated there. Corn was the basic staple of the Indian diet, and the corn was grown at the missions. In addition, the Franciscans directed the growing of fruits and vegetables, as well as extensive ranching. The quantity of foods such as wheat flour shipped by the College (Apostolic College of Santa Cruz de Querétaro) from Saltillo (Coahuila) did not vary from year to year, despite fluctuations in the numbers of Indians on the missions. This suggests that these food items were not exclusively destined for consumption by the Indians.

The College shipped three categories of goods to the missions. The first were goods used in the operation of the mission such as tools, statues, paintings, and other adornments for the churches, and wine and candles used during mass. The second were goods primarily for consumption by the Indians such as tobacco, clothing—which was of primary concern for the missionaries, who wanted to cover the nakedness of the Indians—and foods not produced at the missions such as dried fish from Campeche in the Yucatan Peninsula and dried shrimp eaten on days when meat could not be consumed. The final type were goods to be consumed by the missionaries themselves including expensive spices, chocolate, sugar, rice, and some articles of clothing.

Price fluctuations may have determined the actual quantity and to a certain degree the selection of goods sent from year to year, although the Franciscans sent requests to the College. However, account books (San Juan Bautista and San Bernardo on the Rio Grande River, San Lorenzo, and in the San Antonio area San Antonio, La Purísima Concepción, San Juan Capistrano, and San Francisco de la Espada missions) of goods shipped to the missions summarized in Tables 1.1 and 1.2 do show that for most of the period from 1745 to the early 1770s the Franciscans received a set supply of basic foods. The basic supplies generally included eight to ten *arrobas* (1 arroba = 25 lbs.) of fine and ordinary chocolate, sugar, rice, flour, and sometimes chick peas. The Franciscans also received small quantities of expensive spices. Small variations in the quantity of these goods occurred from year to year, but the Guardian of the College made sure that the Franciscan missionaries received what might be called a basic ration. The supplies sent to San Juan Capistrano in 1752 were typical: 7 arrobas of chocolate; 2 *tercios* (1 tercio = about 6 arrobas); 6 arrobas of sugar; 1 arroba of rice; and 2½ arrobas of chick peas.

In a number of instances the account books registered sharp price increases for goods imported from Spain or elsewhere, such as spices and wine. These increases were particularly evident during the major international wars that involved Spain during the middle eighteenth century: the War of Austrian Succession (1742–1748) and the Seven Years' War (1756–1763). The activities of enemy navies and privateers disrupted trade, while at the same time the Spanish government experimented with dismantling the *flota* system (flotillas of merchant ships

Table 1.1

Selected Commodity Prices in Pesos and Reales, 1745–1772

Year	Sugar arroba	Rice arroba	Ordinary chocolate lb.	Steel arroba	Parras wine barrel	Saltillo flour carga	Tobacco carga
1745	19r	8r	72r		18p	80r	45p
1746	16 1/2r	20r	72r			104r	37p
1747	16 1/2r	8r	64r				50p
1748	16 1/2r	10r		25p			50p
1749	18r	10r	72r	6 1/2p	15 7/8p	80r	
1750	19r	16r		6 1/2p	15 7/8p	104r	65p
1751	18r		73r		23 1/4p	104r	50p
1752	16r	16r	70r	8p			
1753	16r	14r		6 3/4p	19 3/4p	48r	32 1/4p
1754	16r	10r	61r	6 1/2p	21 3/8p	48r	40p
1755	17 1/2r	12r			20p	40r	55p
1756	13r	20r			20p	48r	50p
1757	16r	14r	75r		22 5/8p	64r	
1758	16r	8r	64r		19 3/8p	48r	
1759	16r	9r		9p	19 3/8p	72r	55p
1760	17 1/2r	8r	72r		19 3/8p	72r	55p
1761	17 1/2r	6r		6p		51r	58p
1762	16r	8 1/2r	68r			63r	
1763	16r	10r	64r			39r	45p
1764	18r	6r	64r				44p
1765	16r	7r	60r	7p			
1766	13 1/2r	6r	48r		12 1/8p	40r	
1767	13r	9r	64r	6p	18p		
1768	10r	8r	56r	6p			
1769	10 1/2r	8r	56r	6p			
1770	10r	8 1/2r	60r				
1771	10r	8r	60r				
1772	14r	12r	53r	6p			

Source: Data compiled from mission records. Archivo del Colegio de Santa Cruz de Queretaro, Zelaya, Mexico.

protected by warships) in favor of a system of ships registered in Spain to trade in the Americas. Wine and imported spices, discussed in more detail below, are examples of the war-related increases in prices. Crop failures in different parts of Mexico could also drive prices up on a short-term basis. However, the overall trend shows declining prices for most goods from the 1740s to the early 1770s.

The College routinely shipped wheat flour purchased in Saltillo, a large urban and wheat-growing center in Coahuila, to the Texas missions. The Franciscans did not produce wheat in the San Antonio and Rio Grande missions, and instead focused on corn which was the grain deemed to be suitable for lower-status indigenous folk. This shows that

Table 1.2

Prices of Selected Spices in Reales, 1746–1772

Year	Pepper lb.	Cumin lb.	Clove lb.	Cinnamon lb.
1746				24
1747	24		32	
1748	26	5	64	26
1749	6			
1750	6		44	26 1/2
1751	9			
1752	8 1/2	7	52	
1753	7	9		56
1754	6 1/2	8		36
1755	8	1 1/2		42
1756	11	1	48	42
1757	9			48
1758	13	2		60
1759				56
1760	10	2		72
1762	6	3		
1763	8	2 1/2	40	64
1764	6		34	54
1765	5	3	32	44
1766	5	1		36
1767	5	1	64	36
1769	6 1/2		44	
1770			64	
1772	3			48

Source: Data compiled from mission records. Archivo del Colegio de Santa Cruz de Queretaro, Zelaya, Mexico.

the missions were closely linked to regional markets in northeastern New Spain where wheat flour could be cheaply purchased. Therefore, there was little need for the missions to produce wheat. Moreover, the missions did not sell large quantities of grain to the nearby military garrisons, for that could also be supplied from Saltillo wheat farmers or else local settlers in Texas. This stands in marked contrast to patterns in the California missions, where the Franciscans directed the production of large quantities of wheat for consumption both at the missions and presidios.

The list of goods shipped to the frontier missions also provides insight into the social history of the Franciscan missionaries themselves. Despite serving on an isolated frontier, the Franciscans, many of whom were Spanish natives from well-to-do families, maintained certain dietary standards as shown by the expensive goods they received. The College shipped large quantities of chocolate (chocolate mixed with sugar

Table 1.3

Prices in Reales of Selected Goods Shipped to San Diego Mission, 1774–1811

Year	Wine barrel	Aguardiente barrel	Fine choc. arroba	Ordinary choc. arroba	Steel arroba	Canela lb.	Clove lb.	Yerba de puebla arroba
1774			80	62	52	68	72	
1775			85	52			46	
1776			73	44		56	38	
1777			73	50				
1778				44		48		22
1779			83	44		48		
1780			83	44			48	
1781			83	44				
1782	360		83	44	64	48		
1783	304		83	44		64		
1784	316	320	81	40			64	16
1785	296		85	42				18
1786	252		84	42		64	64	18
1787	264		82	40				24
1788	209		78	42		48	44	40
1789	187		78	36				
1790	202		75	42				20
1791	196		69					38
1792	228		123	100		64		13
1793	293 1/2		77	50		54		12
1794			80	48				16
1795	306		83	27			68	20
1801			82	44	332	24		20

Year							
1802	570		87	44			
1803	231	424	84	44			
1804	424		85	40			40
1805			78				
1806			109				
1807			80	32 1/2	50		
1808			80	32 1/2	64		
1809			90 1/2	24	40	28	
1810			80	36			
1811			80 1/2	36	71		

Source: Untitled account book, for San Diego Mission, of supplies shipped by the Apostolic College of San Fernando to San Diego Mission, "Documentos Para la Historia de Mexico," vol. 18, Archivo General de la Nacion, Mexico, D.F.

Table 1.4

Prices in Reales for Selected Goods Shipped to Santa Clara Mission, 1779–1810

Year	Wine barrel	Aguardiente barrel	Fine choc. arroba	Ordinary choc. arroba	Steel arroba	Rice arroba	Sugar arroba	Clove lb.	Pepper lb.
1779			83	44				40	6
1780			83	44					
1781			80						
1782	360		83	44		16	28		
1783	304							34	8
1784	316				48				
1785		320	81					16	6
1786	252	258	85	42				32	
1787	264		85	40				48	
1788	187	262	82	36					
1789	209	295	78	56				44	
1790	202	300	78	42	48			33	5 1/2
1791	206	358	75		56				
1792	228	284	78						
1793	379		119 1/2	41 1/2	45			32 1/2	10
1794	224	280	74		45			64 1/2	15
1795	303	319	124 1/2		69			112	10
1801	800		88	44 1/2		11			
1802	1,124		87	45		17			
1803	231	428	82	45	50	16	25 1/2		5
1804	848	275					28		
1805	273	275					25 1/2		
1806	288					17 1/2			
1807			108	44		17			8
1808	448	376	80	32		15 1/2		28	
1809	456		90 1/2	32		25 1/2	23 1/2		
1810	297	349	80			24	15		

Source: Untitled account book, for Santa Clara Mission, of supplies shipped by the Apostolic College of San Fernando to Santa Clara Mission, "Documentos Para la Historia de Mexico," vol. 18, Archivo General de la Nacion, Mexico, D.F.

Table 1.5

Prices in Reales of Selected Goods Shipped to San José Mission, 1800–1812

Year	Wine barrel	Aguardiente barrel	Fine choc. arroba	Ordinary choc. arroba	Rice tercio	Sugar tercio	Yerba de puebla arroba	Fideo arroba
1800	408		81	44 1/2	76			
1802	584		87					
1803	231		82	48	56		20	
1804	848	592	63	40	123		20	
1805	273				118			
1806	288			45				
1807	250		80 1/2	32 1/2		202		26 1/2
1808	297		90 1/2	32 1/2				
1809			80	32 1/2	95	175		20
1810	309							
1811					149			
1812			61 1/2	31		88		24

Source: Untitled account book, for San José Mission, of supplies shipped by the Apostolic College of San Fernando to San José Mission, "Documentos Para la Historia de Mexico," vol. 18, Archivo General de la Nacion, Mexico, D.F.

and cinnamon similar to chocolate still sold in Mexico today), sugar, and *piloncillo* (brown sugar cones) in quantities that indicate that a supply for an entire year was being provided to the Franciscans. In most years the Franciscans ordered between 200 and 250 pounds of various grades of chocolate. Moreover, the Franciscans also received expensive imported and locally produced spices such as clove, cinnamon, black pepper, cumin, and oregano to flavor what otherwise must have been a bland diet. Most Mexicans could not afford to buy these spices. The College purchased spices for the missionaries even during periods of elevated prices, such as during the War of Austrian Succession (1742–1748) when prices for imported spices experienced sharp increases and in one instance doubled from one year to the next. In 1747, for example, a pound of clove cost 32 reales, but then doubled to 64 reales in the following year. Similarly, in 1748 a pound of pepper cost 26 reales, but then dropped to six reales in the following year. Cinnamon prices rose to as high as 72 reales a pound in 1760 during the Seven Years' War, but were as low as 36 reales in the late 1760s following the conclusion of hostilities.

The pattern in the California missions was different from that in Texas, and the California missions played a different role in economic development. In the early 1770s, the Franciscan leaders of the Apostolic College of San Fernando worked out a formal agreement with the viceregal government to supply the military garrisons (presidios) with food, leather goods, and crude textiles. The Franciscans harnessed Indian labor to not only provide food for the Indians living on the missions, but also to subsidize the cost to the Spanish government of the colonization of California by significantly reducing the actual price of supplying the military garrisons. The colonization of California occurred at the beginning of the so-called Bourbon reforms, a major fiscal reorganization that attempted to increase revenues while at the same time cutting costs wherever possible.

Four classes of documents contain information on the supply of the California missions and the role of the missions in the economic activity of the region. They include the account of the goods shipped by the College to the missions, the account books of transactions at the missions themselves, annual reports that summarized spiritual and temporal activities at each of the missions, and accounts of the food and other goods supplied to the presidios and *escoltas* (military detachment) assigned to each mission. The California missions were more self-sufficient than the Texas establishments. Agricultural production included a wider variety of crops including corn, wheat, barley, and *frijol* (pinto beans), in addition to fruits and vegetables. As noted above, the Franciscans directed the production of wheat for supply to the presidios as well as for consumption in the missions. The cost of shipping wheat from the closest producing regions in northern or central Mexico would have been prohibitively high. Production levels and the numbers of livestock were also considerably higher in California than in Texas.

The annual reports most commonly reported the supply of equipment for the mission, such as statues and other items for the churches. The on-site account books list additional items not produced on the missions and shipped from central Mexico. One Santa Cruz mission account book, for example, listed fine cloth, cotton cloth, gunpowder, iron, tobacco and tobacco products, chocolate, sugar and *panocha* (sugar cone), and *aguardiente* (cane brandy) and *mescal*, both alcoholic beverages. The Franciscans sold goods imported from Mexico and locally produced goods to individual soldiers and settlers, who maintained accounts with the missions. The account books also included references to the hiring of Indians to soldiers and settlers, with payment made to the Franciscans. The Franciscans also supplied large quantities of goods to the presidios and detachments at the missions, and maintained detailed accounts of these transactions called *sumininistraciones*. Wheat and other grains topped the list of goods supplied to the military, but the Franciscans also provided leather goods including shoes and crude textiles. In some instances the Franciscans supplied a tenth to as much as a fifth of total mission grain production to the military.

The accounts of goods shipped to the California missions show both similar and dissimilar patterns to the accounts for the Texas missions. The Franciscans ordered a large variety of goods produced in Mexico and in Spain: wine and aguardiente came from Spain, and in some instances the accounts specified Catalonia as the source of the aguardiente and Málaga and Jerez wine; from Mexico came *yerba de Puebla,* most likely a medicinal tea; *arroz de la costa,* rice most likely from tropical coastal regions such as modern Guerrero; *leche de Michoacán*; and *palo de campeche* and brazilwood used for producing dye for textiles. The accounts also include items not found in the Texas records, highlighting some differences between the missions in the two regions. The Franciscans in California ordered munitions, which included the gunpowder listed in the on-site Santa Cruz mission account book cited above. The missionaries also ordered mercury and mercury pills used to treat syphilis, a major medical problem among the Indians living on the missions.

The accounts also reveal that the Spanish government, involved in protracted wars in the late eighteenth and early nineteenth centuries, was unable to supply the same level of support for the Franciscans stationed in the California missions as had been the case in Texas. Spain participated in the American Revolutionary War (1775–1783) and the French Revolutionary and Napoleonic wars (1792–1815), generally in opposition to the British. After 1792 in particular, the fiscal state of the Spanish government was precarious at best. Wartime price increases also significantly undermined the ability of the Franciscans in California to obtain the same level of expensive specialized foods as had the Texas missionaries at an earlier period. The California missionaries imported fewer and smaller quantities of expensive spices, and in some instances imported chili powder as a less expensive alternative. Moreover, particularly after 1790, they ordered less chocolate. Finally, volatile shifts in wine prices ate into the money available for the purchase of supplies, and forced the missionaries to do with less (see Figures 1.1 and 1.2).

The most dramatic increase in wine prices occurred in 1801, 1802, 1803, and 1804. In 1801 the missionaries stationed at Santa Clara paid 800 reales for a barrel of wine. (To place this figure into context, in the ten years between 1786 and 1795, the cost of a barrel of wine averaged only 245 reales.) In 1802, the price rose even higher to 1,124 reales, and in that year the Franciscans ordered relatively little in the way of other supplies. The temporary end of hostilities in Europe in 1803 lowered the price of wine back to 231 reales per barrel, but the price shot up to 848 reales in the following year with the resumption of hostilities. The price of imported aguardiente also rose and fell with the ebb and flow of the wars in Europe, as recorded in the accounts for San José and San Juan Bautista missions. In 1803, the barrel of aguardiente cost 428 reales, rising to 592 in the following year, and then dropping to 275 in 1805.

How did the Franciscans respond to the wartime price fluctuations? In the short run they had to reduce the requests to conform to the fixed amount provided by the government. The Franciscans may have also attempted to increase wine and aguardiente production at the missions: Spanish legislation already prohibited wine production in Mexico, to prevent competition for wines produced in Spain. The missionaries also began to trade illegally with foreigners who visited the California coast in search of fur-bearing marine mammals and trade in hides and tallow.

Figure 1.1 **Price of Wine Shipped to San Diego Mission, 1782–1804**

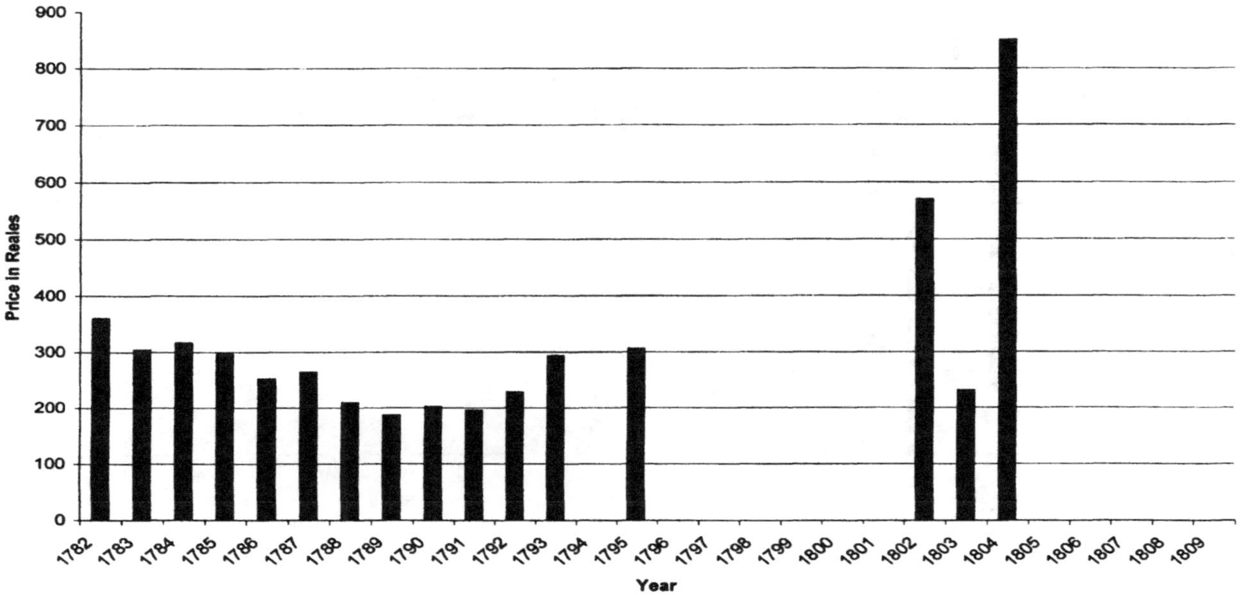

Source: Untitled account book, for San Diego Mission, of supplies shipped by the Apostolic College of San Fernando to San Diego Mission, "Documentos Para la Historia de Mexico," vol. 18, Archivo General de la Nacion, Mexico, D.F.

Figure 1.2 **Price of Wine Shipped to Santa Clara Mission, 1782–1809**

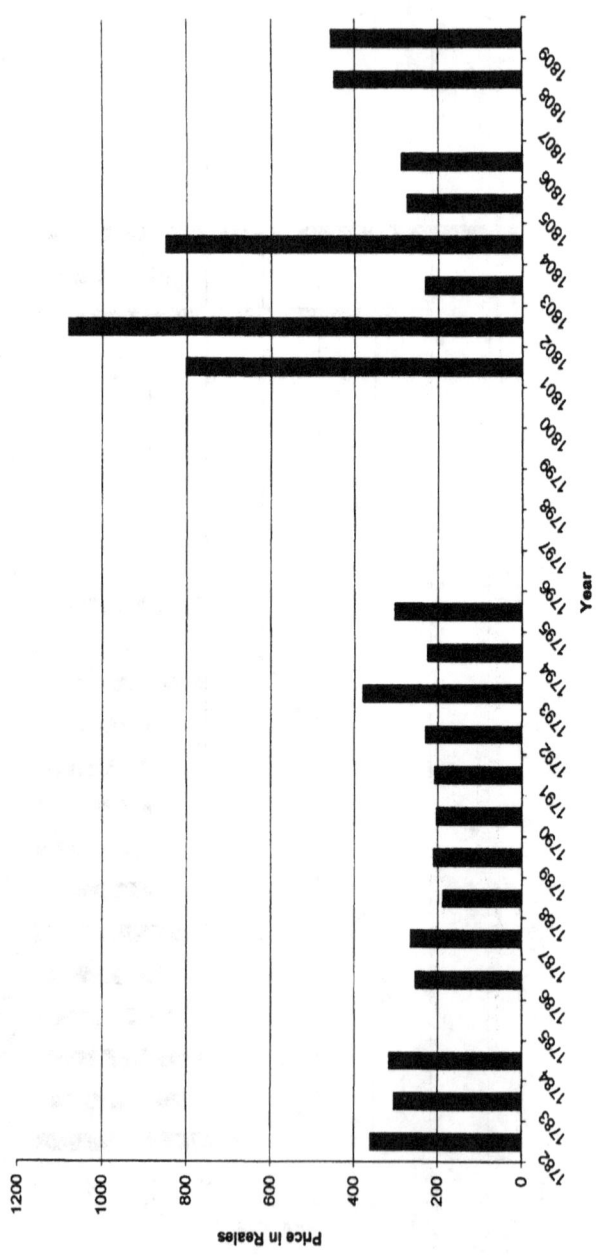

Source: Untitled account book, for Santa Clara Mission, of supplies shipped by the Apostolic College of San Fernando to Santa Clara Mission, "Documentos Para la Historia de Mexico," vol. 18, Archivo General de la Nacion, Mexico, D.F.

The origins of the so-called "hide and tallow" trade can perhaps be traced back to the first years of the nineteenth century, characterized by the volatility in certain prices for goods deemed necessary for the functioning of the missions, such as wine.

The outbreak of the independence wars in central Mexico (1810–1821) caused the cessation of the supply of goods from central Mexico to the missions. Available funds went to fighting the wars, and the activities of insurgents cut off supply routes to California. The Franciscans responded by expanding the volume of illegal trade with foreigners who visited the California coast. But this trade really developed in the crisis years of price volatility during the wars at the beginning of the new century.

Local and Regional Markets

The mission economies did not develop in isolation, and in several frontier regions the missionaries and Indians participated in local/regional markets through the sale of food and other supplies, and labor. The Franciscans stationed in New Mexico and the Pueblo Indians sold goods produced at the missions, and also were involved in trade with surrounding tribes from the Plains. In the seventeenth and eighteenth centuries periodic fairs (*rescates/ferias*) took place where Indians such as the Comanches, Utes, Navajos, and Apaches exchanged hides, tallow, dried meat, and salt for a variety of goods including grain, livestock, blankets, pottery, turquoise, and European goods including firearms and gunpowder. The most important fairs were at Pecos and Taos, but there were others at Picuris, Santa Clara, Jémez, and Acoma.

Items from the trade with other Indian groups also figured into trade to Chihuahua, which grew toward the end of the eighteenth century. New Mexicans exported a variety of goods to Chihuahua, and this trade changed during the last two decades of the eighteenth century. Until about the 1770s, New Mexico exported deerskins and buffalo hides, and blankets and other textiles. In the 1780s and 1790s, sheep and woolen blankets became the mainstay of the New Mexico–Chihuahua trade, but other livestock and *punche* (a tobacco substitute) were also important. Additionally, Pueblo Indians mass produced pottery for sale in Chihuahua, under the direction of settlers rather than the missionaries. This mass production diluted the quality of the pottery. Pueblo Indians participated in regional markets through the production of woolen blankets and pottery.

The Jesuit and Franciscan missionaries stationed on the Pimería Alta missions of northern Sonora actively participated in the developing regional market that was dominated by mining. In addition to the mission communities established by Jesuit missionaries in the seventeenth and eighteenth centuries, there were mining camps, farming hamlets, and cattle and sheep ranches in northern Sonora. The population of the Sonora frontier was unstable, fluid, and highly mobile. A population of professional miners and fortune hunters tested their luck in a series of mining strikes throughout the province. News of a mining strike set hundreds of thousands of people in motion, drawn to the prospect of quick wealth in the new mining districts, often depopulating older communities. The mobility of the population challenged the colonial objective of the development of stable populations on the frontier and created a problem conceptualized by royal officials as vagabondage. The mobility of the Sonora population also posed problems for the Jesuit and later the Franciscan missionaries. The Franciscans attempted to slowly bring their charges into Spanish society without being contaminated by what they considered to be the vices of a racially mixed population. But the population categorized as being of mixed ancestry could not be made to stay in one place or be prevented from establishing contact with the Indian converts living in the missions.

The history of the settlement of Sonora in the seventeenth and eighteenth centuries was characterized by a series of boom and bust mining cycles, and the mobility of a small population of miners that tried their luck with each new gold and silver discovery. What differentiated the pattern of migration in the late eighteenth century, stimulated by economic growth related to the Bourbon reforms, from the earlier period was not the mobility of people living in the northern frontier, but the greater scale. The expansion of internal markets led to an intensification of commercial agriculture, and population growth in the corporate indigenous communities placed greater pressure on a limited land base. The frontier population experienced growth through short- and long-distance migration and natural reproduction, and a relatively larger number of people were on the move when compared to the previous century.

The number of people attracted to newly discovered mineral deposits increased during the course of the eighteenth century, and by the last third of the century involved thousands. The example of the La Cieneguilla mining district located in the southern Pimería Alta is a case in point. A military patrol discovered placer gold deposits at La

Cieneguilla in 1771, and news of the richness of the deposits soon attracted large numbers of fortune hunters. By January of 1773, some 7,000 people reportedly lived in the La Cieneguilla mining district. Moreover, a sizable number of Yaqui and other Sonoran Indians came to work in the mines on a seasonal basis. From the 1770s until the 1840s, the population of the mining district fluctuated. People left or came with the exhaustion of known deposits or the discovery of new placers, until the last settlement in the district was abandoned as a result of raids by hostile Indians and 49ers on their way to the California gold fields. In 1778, the population of the mining district was down to 775, but grew to 5,000 people in the first years of the nineteenth century, only to decline again to 838 at the end of 1816.

The growing number of mining strikes in Sonora contributed to the growth of a dynamic local market economy in produce, livestock, and leather products, as well as a labor market. The establishment of military garrisons in central and northern Sonora created secondary markets for goods produced locally. Farming and ranching communities developed in response to the growth in the local market, and directly led to an accelerated rate of usurpation of mission lands. Moreover, settlers moved into the mission communities in the Pimería Alta and other parts of Sonora, and marginalized or completely displaced the Indian populations.

Geographically isolated until American merchant ships began visiting in the early nineteenth century, the economy of Alta California supplied the basic subsistence needs of the missions, military garrisons, and small number of settlers. The province never found profitable exports until American merchants began buying cattle hides for the shoe factories of New England and tallow for the production of soap and candles. In the early nineteenth century American and Russian hunters came to the coast of both Californias in search of sea otters and fur seals, but the missionaries and settlers participated only marginally in the fur trade in the nineteenth-century.

In the 1780s, the Spanish government attempted to promote the development of a trade in otter pelts to be collected in California for export to China via the Manila galleon. The granting of a monopoly license for the export of otter pelts stimulated hunting for animals under the direction of the Franciscans. Correspondance between the missionaries in California and their superiors in Mexico City show that some Franciscans continued to collect pelts for export even after the monopoly license expired, but this was on a relatively minor scale. The government also promoted hemp production, but this initiative never resulted in the development of exports. Hemp planted at several missions satisfied local demand for fiber. The high cost of transportation prevented the Franciscans from developing viable exports.

The economy of the California missions was oriented toward two objectives: the supply of the thousands of Indians congregated on the missions; and the supply of food, leather goods, and textiles to the soldiers stationed on the presidios. The Franciscan missionaries who staffed the Alta California missions contributed to the colonization of the region by exploiting Indian labor to produce large agricultural surpluses and large herds of livestock used to subsidize the cost to the government of maintaining military garrisons in the region. The Franciscans supplied food, leather goods, and clothing to the presidios at a cost that was significantly lower than that of supplying the presidios from central Mexico via the port of San Blas in Sinaloa. When the first mission was established in San Diego in 1769, the Franciscans had a mandate from Visitor-General José de Galvez to colonize Alta California, but the mandate did not include Franciscan control over mission temporalities (Indian labor and all economic activity in the missions). The Franciscans were not given control over mission temporalities when they assumed control of the Baja California missions from the recently expelled Jesuits, and occupied Alta California under the same conditions.

In 1773 Junipero Serra, O.F.M., father-president and architect of the Alta California missions, signed an agreement with the viceregal government in Mexico City. Under the terms of the agreement the government granted the Franciscans control over mission temporalities in exchange for selling food and other goods to the military garrisons at rates set in an official price list put together by the governor of the province. Over the next sixty years the Franciscans supplied food, clothing, and leather goods to the military. However, in granting the missions a monopoly over the supply of the military, the government contributed to the economic stagnation of the three pueblos established in the province. The settlers fully participated in the economic development of Alta California only following the closing of the missions after 1834 and the distribution of former mission lands and livestock to prominent settlers and local politicians through hundreds of land grants.

As noted above, the Franciscans kept detailed records of supplies provided to the military in documents called *suministraciones* that served as the basis for accounts presented to the royal treasury in Mexico City.

Additionally, they maintained separate account books for transactions with individual soldiers and settlers that included sales of food, textiles, and leather goods, and the rental of Indian laborers, and also recorded the large sales of supplies to the military. The account books also recorded contracts with the *mayordomos* (overseers). Several examples provide a sense of the nature and scale of the transactions. As a result of the outbreak of the Mexican independence wars in 1810, the military became even more dependent on the missions for supplies often secured through trade with foreign merchants who visited the California coast in increasing numbers. In 1797, the Franciscans stationed at Santa Cruz mission provided planting seed to the settlers only recently arrived from Nueva Galicia (modern Jalisco, Mexico) to establish the Villa de Branciforte. In the same year the members of the escolta received grain, lard, and cattle on the hoof. In 1822, the value of supplies provided to San Francisco presidio totaled 2,090 pesos. Supplies provided included grain, frijol, lard, and 184 pairs of shoes. The arrival of foreign ships also appears in the accounts: in 1817, the British ship *Traveler* bought supplies at Santa Cruz mission and in 1823 the Russian ship *Bulsakoff* bought wheat and lard from Santa Clara mission.

True market economies failed to develop in both Texas and Baja California. Settlers in San Antonio and east Texas did trade with Louisiana and the neighboring provinces of northern Mexico. However, the Franciscan missionaries stationed at the missions did not participate in this trade in a significant way. They may have sold some surpluses locally, but largely relied on the supply system for the goods that they could not have produced locally. The most significant interactions between the Franciscans and local settlers involved disputes over land, particularly rangeland, and efforts by settlers to gain access to Indian labor. The Jesuit, Franciscan, and Dominican missionaries stationed on the Baja California missions operated at a level of self-sufficiency, and at times received subsidies from neighboring regions such as Sinaloa and Sonora. There was one instance where the Baja California establishments contributed to colonial policy objectives. This was in 1769, when José de Galvez ordered the Franciscan missionaries to provide jerked meat and other supplies for the expedition organized for the occupation of Alta California. This order significantly depleted the herds of mission livestock carefully built up over decades by the Jesuits, only recently expelled from the Spanish empire. In both cases, true market economies developed following the demise of the mission system.

Chapter 2

The Building of the Missions

Some of the enduring remains of the missions established on the frontier of northern Mexico are the buildings. In many instances, most of the structures associated with a mission complex have disappeared, except for the church. The most famous mission architecture is found in California and is characterized by arches and red tile roofs. This style, drawn from Mediterranean architectural tradition, generated a popular style of architecture in the 1920s called "Mission Style." This built upon what can be called the "mystique" of the California missions and the discovery, or more properly rediscovery, of the ruins of the mission building complexes by such groups as the Landmarks Club in California at the end of the nineteenth century. The crumbling ruins evoked a romantic Spanish heritage that appealed to Anglo-American society.

 The construction of churches and other structures occupied large numbers of native workers over extended periods of time, and when completed the building complexes represented functional communities with granaries and grist mills, workshops, and housing for the indigenous converts in addition to the church and apartments for the missionaries. The physical organization of the mission building complexes differed in the regions studied here, and those differences illuminate a number of important issues. For example, the inclusion of military features in some mission complexes points to problems with hostile indigenous groups. The location of the complex in relation to indigenous settlements provides clues to the level of control that the missionaries exercised over the natives. Finally, in some instances the missionaries included measures of social control in the mission building complexes, such as enclosure of Indian housing by walls.

This chapter examines the construction of the mission building complexes. The documentation available is different for the regions studied here, and is most complete for the California missions built in the late eighteenth century. In the last years of the eighteenth century the Spanish government required more frequent and detailed reports on the progress of the missions. The practice had generally been for the periodic preparation of reports that sometimes contained information on the structures that made up the mission complex. In the last three decades of the century the government required the missionaries to draft yearly reports that included information on building projects. Therefore, the information on the later missions is much more complete. The first area considered is New Mexico.

The Buildings of the New Mexico Missions

The building complexes of the New Mexico missions most closely resembled the corporate indigenous communities of central Mexico. The Franciscans generally built massive fortress convents in the seventeenth century, and then in the eighteenth century following the Pueblo Revolt of 1680 the scale of construction was smaller because of decline in the size of the indigenous populations. The imposing size of the seventeenth-century fortress convents can best be seen at Abo, Quarai, and Humanas, all located east of Albuquerque on the edge of the Staked Plains in the so-called Salinas province, and Giusewa (Jémez) northwest of Albuquerque. The Franciscans directed the construction of all four fortress convents in the early and mid-seventeenth century, and the missionaries ordered the abandonment of all four before the Pueblo Revolt of 1680. The Franciscans had the churches built on a large scale with tall and thick walls, and, as is still visible at the Giusewa ruins (Jémez Springs), added defensive features to the churches such as lookout towers. The convents could also be used for defense in case of attack. The fortress convents, however, incorporated Pueblo construction techniques and appearance.

The Franciscans had the fortress convents built outside of and adjoining the Pueblo apartment complexes. Symbolically, the fortress convent sat outside of and on the margins of the Pueblo world. From the Franciscan perspective the location of the fortress convent symbolized the reorientation of the Pueblo world to a new public space centered on the central plaza of the new mission communities, facing the new sa-

30 CHAPTER 2

Map 2.1 **Nuevo México**

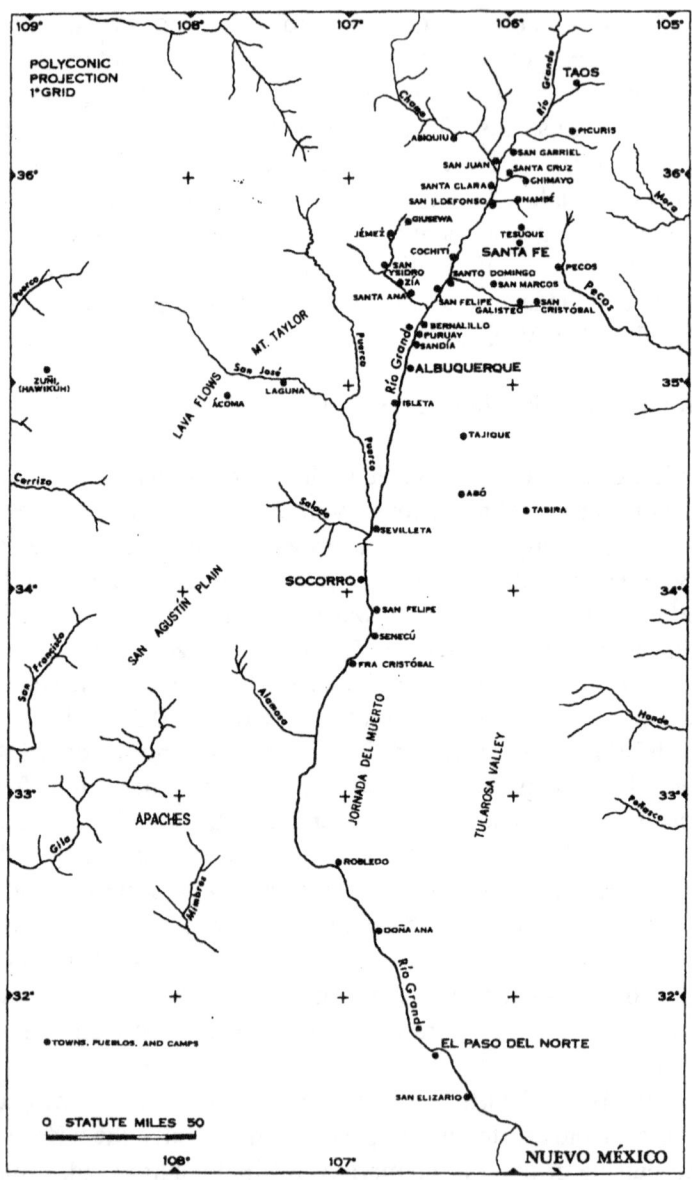

Source: Adapted from John Francis Bannon, *The Spanish Borderlands Frontier, 1513–1821*. Albuquerque: University of New Mexico Press, 1974, 11. Reprinted by permission of the publisher.

cred space of the church. As was also the case with Spanish towns built in the Americas on the grid plan, the plaza became the center of the community. The fortress convent occupied one side of the new plaza, and was built to be the most imposing structure. The sixteenth-century missionaries in central Mexico inserted their presence into the corporate indigenous communities, and built the fortress convents on the new plaza that became the center of the communities. However, the Franciscans in New Mexico failed to make the fortress convent the center of Pueblo life, and Pueblo communal spaces such as the kiva survived despite Franciscan anti-idolatry campaigns and other efforts to stamp out traditional religion and culture.

Following the Pueblo revolt and the restoration of Spanish rule, the scale of construction of churches and convents was smaller. The continued decline in the size of the Pueblo population was a factor, and the restored Franciscan missions tread lighter on traditional Pueblo culture. One of the first tasks of the Franciscans was to direct the reconstruction of structures damaged during and following the Pueblo revolt. As was the case at Pecos, the new churches were generally smaller. The Franciscans built the new Pecos church inside of the foundations of the late seventeenth-century church destroyed in 1680. In terms of style, the eighteenth-century structures were similar to the structures of the previous century, only built on a smaller scale.

Sonora

The Jesuit and Franciscan missionaries directed the construction of building complexes that became the center of new communities. The Jesuits established the missions at existing indigenous settlements, but the church built on the new plaza became the focus of the community. The natives built new houses along the plaza. The church and convent became the point of reference for the reorganization of native society. The style of architecture was European with little or no visible indigenous influence in design or decoration. The structures that survive today date primarily to the late eighteenth century, and the most impressive is the twin tower San Xavier del Bac located just south of Tucson, Arizona. The surviving churches contained either neobaroque or classical designs, and were built on an impressive scale. The natives built new houses adjoining the plaza, symbolizing the birth of new communities.

32 CHAPTER 2

Map 2.2 **Sonora**

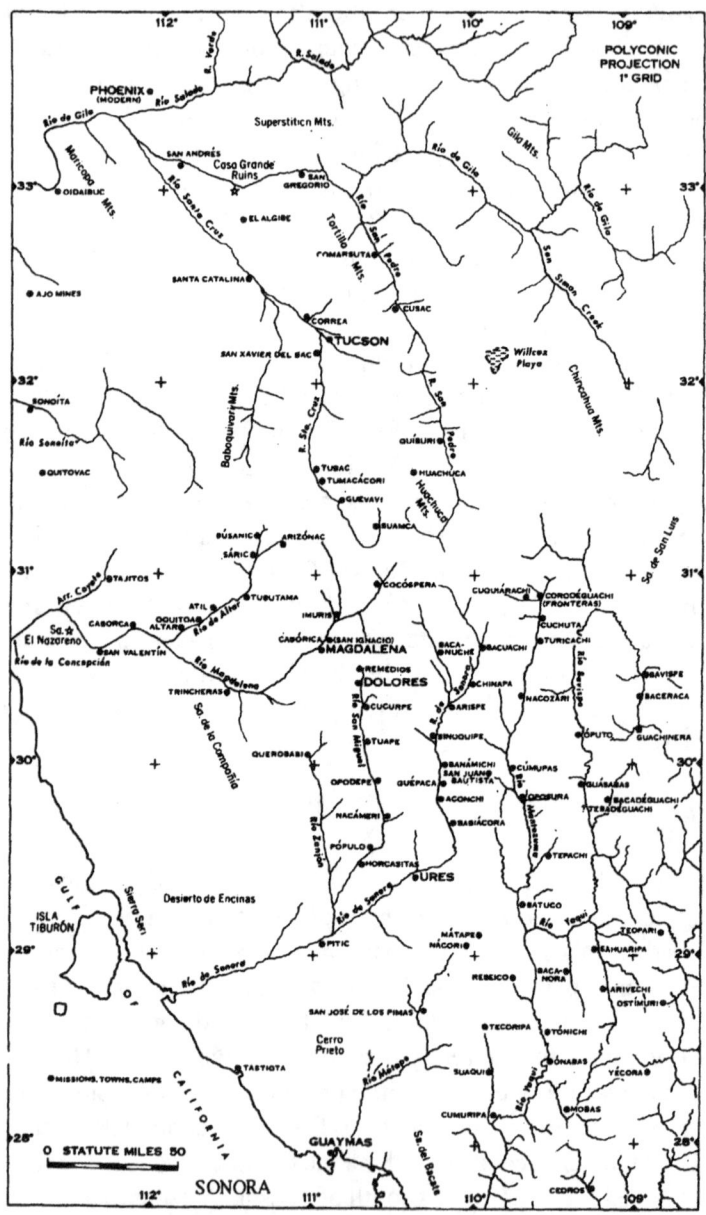

Source: Adapted from John Francis Bannon, *The Spanish Borderlands Frontier, 1513–1821.* Albuquerque: University of New Mexico Press, 1974, Pimeriá Alta, 66. Reprinted by permission of the publisher.

Texas

The Franciscans established some thirty missions in Texas, most of which closed after only several years. There were two styles of architecture and organization of the mission communities. The east Texas missions established among the sedentary Caddoes and Orcoquisacs operated for some fifty to sixty years. Several maps of presidios prepared by Nicolás Lafora in the mid-1760s also pictured the missions that adjoined the military garrisons. The missions, located in the east Texas pine forests, were built of wood plastered inside and out, and were surrounded by palisade walls. The native population continued to live in their villages, and generally failed to build new villages at the missions. This reflected the failure of the Franciscans to convert or acculturate the natives.

The other missions located in west central Texas evolved over a longer period of time, and became the focal point of new communities built from scratch. The longest lasting of these missions were the five establishments located within close proximity of each other in the area of modern San Antonio, and the missions established for the Karankawas and neighboring groups on the Lower San Antonio River and nearby streams. In the 1760s, the Franciscans operated short-lived missions for the Lipan Apaches on the Nueces River, and archaeologists have excavated the building complex of one of the Apache missions.

Hostile indigenous groups raided the missions in central and west Texas, and the Franciscans designed the building complexes for defense. In the first stages of construction buildings were of wood or wattle and daub, but were replaced with permanent structures of stone or adobe. As was the case in the other missions on the frontier of northern Mexico, the church was the largest, most imposing building in the complex, and the size of the church impressed upon the natives the grandeur of the new religion. Walls surrounded the mission, and the walls incorporated defensive features such as bastions and rifle holes cut into the walls at each of the gates leading into the mission. Small apartments for the indigenous families occupied the interior side of the defensive walls, and workshops and granaries also occupied space along the walls or else were located within the walls. Some activities occurred outside of the walls, such as farming and tending the herds of livestock, and a number of missions operated ranches at some distance from the main mission complex. Archaeologists have excavated the fortified compound of one of the ranches and identified defensive elements similar to those

Map 2.3 Texas and Northern Mexico

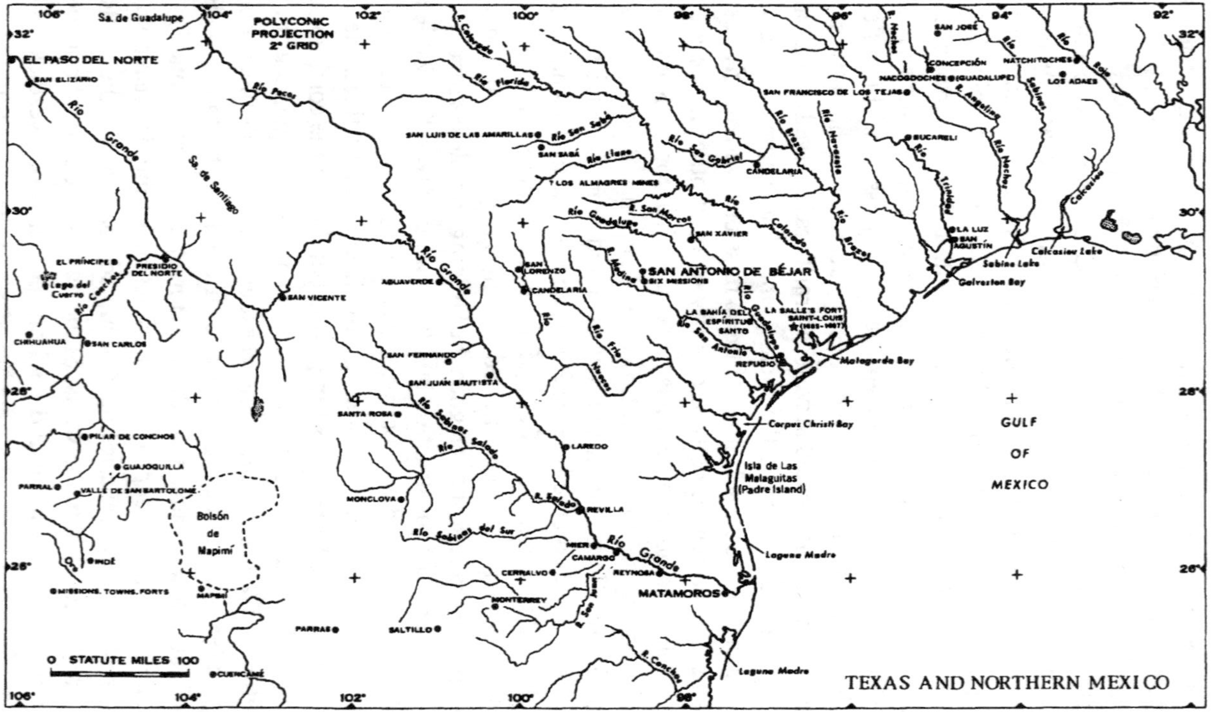

Source: Adapted from John Francis Bannon, *The Spanish Borderlands Frontier, 1513–1821.* Albuquerque: University of New Mexico Press, 1974, Coahuila, Nuevo Léon, Nuevo Santander, and Texas, 113. Reprinted by permission of the publisher.

of the main mission compounds. However, at night the indigenous population returned to the mission complex for protection. The Franciscans built large imposing European-style churches incorporating baroque or classical elements.

Baja and Alta California

The information available on the mission buildings in Baja and Alta California is more detailed and complete, allowing for a more in-depth discussion. The architecture and form of the mission complexes in Baja California was different between the Jesuits and Franciscans. This was related in part to the ecology of the southern and northern parts of the peninsula, as well as the size of the indigenous population. The development of the mission complexes went through stages, with temporary structures replaced by more permanent buildings. But the configuration of the mission compounds changed following the establishment of missions in the northern part of the peninsula. The first period comprises the Jesuit (1697–1768) and brief Franciscan periods (1768–1773) during which time the missions were first under minimal government control until 1768 and later under greater government control when the peninsula reverted to the jurisdiction of authorities appointed by the crown. The brief five-year Franciscan tenure on the peninsula missions coincided with the visitation of José de Galvez, who experimented with and modified policy in the peninsula as in the rest of New Spain. Changes initiated under Galvez in 1768 and 1769 did not necessarily have a lasting impact on the Baja California missions, but the different approach to Spain's colonial policies in Mexico generally known as the Bourbon Reforms was in ways reflected in the development of mission building complexes. It is these changes that are also documented in this section.

As elsewhere, the church was always the dominant structure at the mission community. A series of reports and inventories recorded the dimensions of the mission churches in varas (1 vara = 0.838 meters). The most impressive were the stone church at Loreto built in the 1750s that measured 56 x 7 varas, the longest in the peninsula; the stone church at San Francisco Javier completed between 1744 and 1758; the stone churches at Mulege and Comondu, built about the same time that the Jesuits brought skilled workers to the peninsula to launch a major church-building campaign; and finally the stone church at San Ignacio begun at the end of the Jesuit period but only completed in the 1780s.

36 CHAPTER 2

Map 2.4a **Baja California, North**

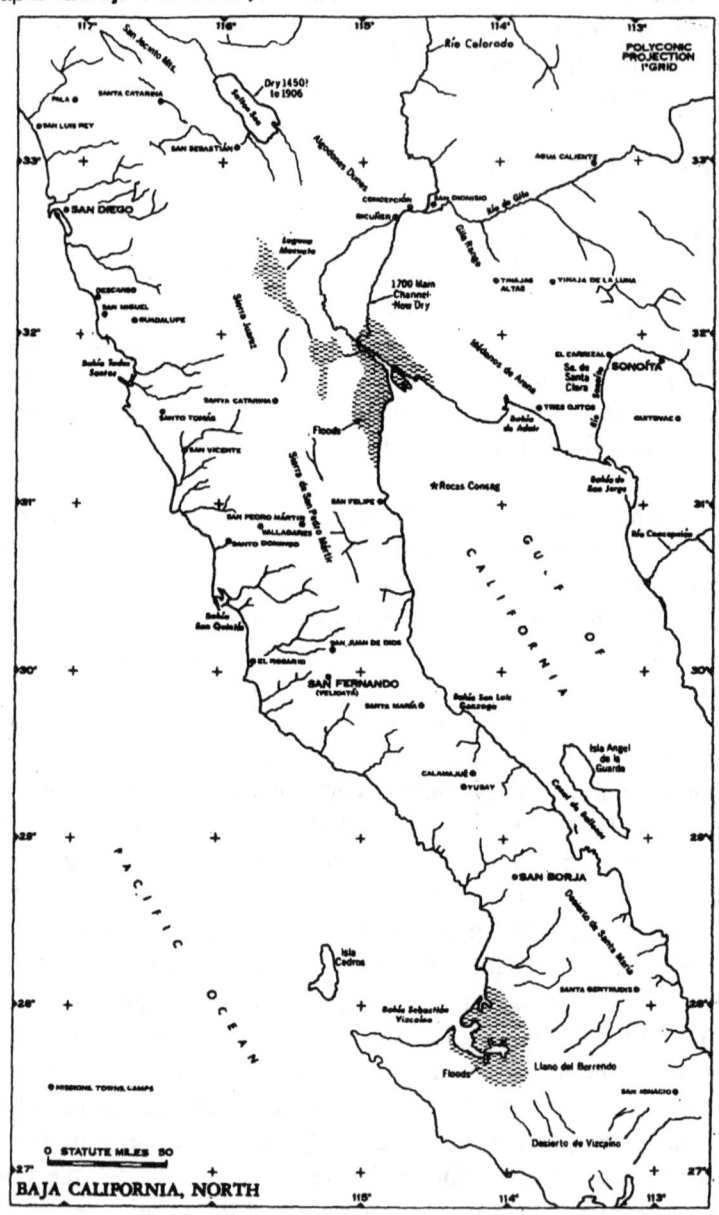

Source: Maps 2.4a and 2.4b are adapted from John Francis Bannon, *The Spanish Borderlands Frontier, 1513–1821*. Albuquerque: University of New Mexico Press, 1974, Baja California South, Baja California North, 144, 145. Reprinted by permission of the publisher.

Map 2.4b **Baja California, South**

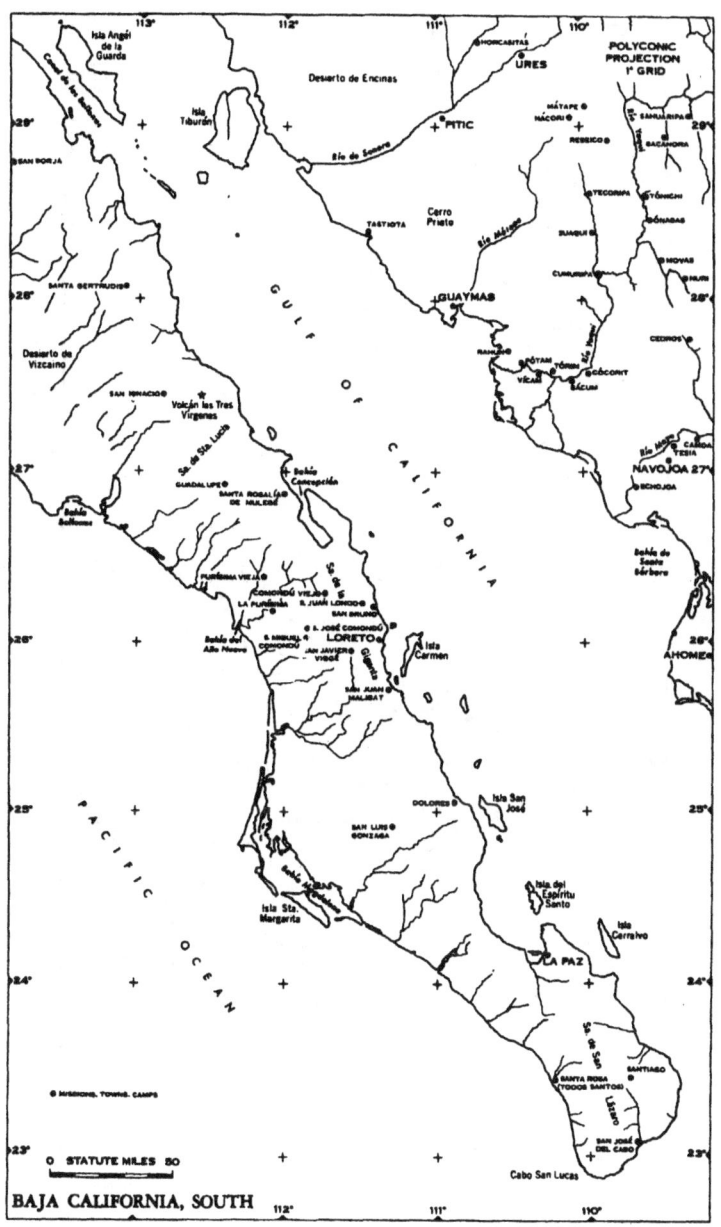

Map 2.5 **Alta California**

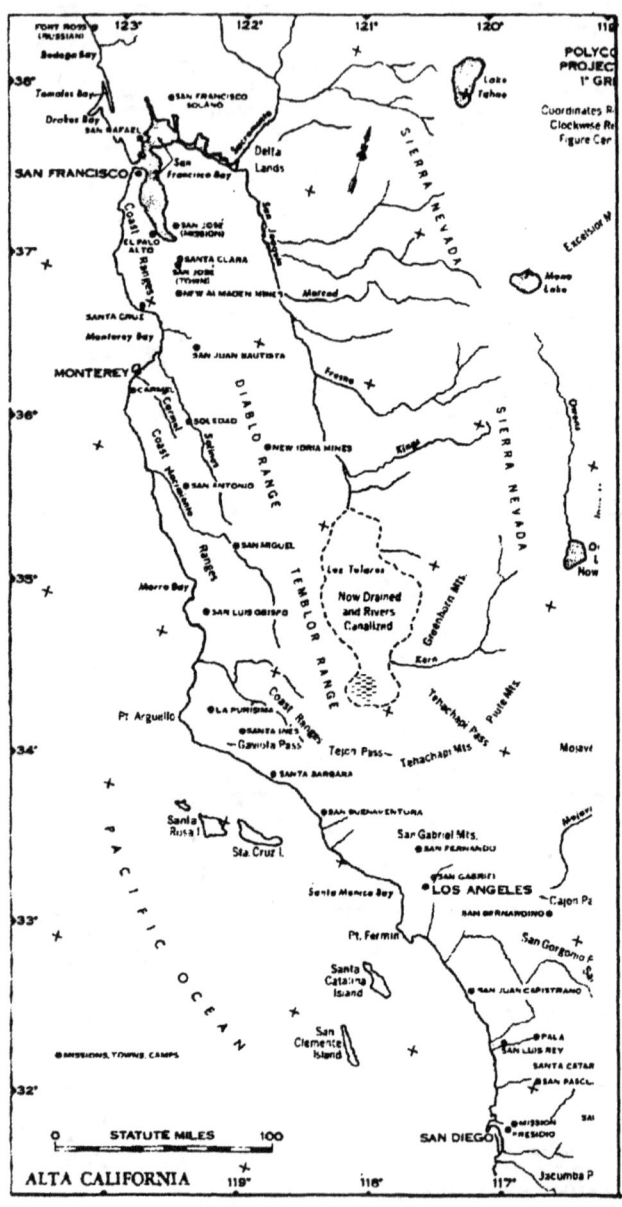

Source: Adapted from John Frances Bannon, *The Spanish Borderlands Frontier, 1513–1821.* Albuquerque: University of New Mexico Press, 1974, 165. Reprinted by permission of the publisher.

The full extent of the development by Jesuits and Franciscans of the mission building complexes can be reconstructed. The first example in San José de Comondu, established in 1708. Between 1708 and 1736, an adobe church and residence for the missionaries built of stone set in mud were built. In 1736, the Jesuits relocated the mission to a new site, and directed the development of a complex that included an adobe church, a residence for the missionary built of the same material, a store room, and dormitories for single women and single men. In addition, a new irrigation system was developed with *acequias* (irrigation ditches), small reservoirs, and a type of terraced garden.

From about 1754 to 1760, the Jesuits directed the construction of a new stone church at Comondu as part of a major campaign to build larger churches at a number of older missions. Joseph de Utrera, S.J., visited Comondu in January 1755, and reported on the construction of the three-nave stone church that was to have an arched ceiling. He reported that work had already progressed on the central nave, but the two outside naves had not advanced much.

An inventory prepared in 1773 in anticipation of the transfer of jurisdiction of the peninsula missions from the Franciscans to the Dominicans provides additional information on the types of structures that made up Comondu mission. In addition to the stone three-nave church, there was a spacious residence for the missionaries built of the same material that also contained offices. Other structures included several granaries and storerooms, a forge, weaving room, tack room, and shoe shop. The Dominicans made few changes to the existing building complex, but did add several structures. Extant annual reports from the 1790s record additional building activities at Comondu. In 1796, the Dominicans directed the construction of a dormitory with a patio for single men, and nine houses for as many Indian families, each measuring 5 x 4 varas. Two years later, in 1798, foundations were laid for a new structure with dimensions of 19 x 6 varas, and a new corral was built.

The second example of a mission building complex is San Francisco de Borja, established in 1762. In the 1773 inventory of the mission, Fermín Francisco de Lasuen, O.F.M. described the structures at the mission. Lasuen had replaced the adobe church built by the Jesuits with a larger structure of the same material that had with a stone arch and roof of tules with packed earth covering roof beams. To the side of the church were three wings of rooms that formed a square. On one side was the residence of the missionaries, on the second side two workrooms, and on the third a hall.

Other structures at the mission site included a kitchen, two infirmaries, a granary, wine cellar, and tack room. Lasuen's church remained in use until replaced by the Dominicans in 1801 by a stone church and a stone residence for the missionaries.

Detailed inventories prepared in 1773 and 1774 with the change in jurisdiction from the Franciscans to the Dominicans provide additional details on the building complexes at the Baja California missions at one point in time at the end of the Franciscan period. San Francisco Javier (established 1699) had a stone church as well as a stone residence for the missionaries. There were also ten adobe structures most likely used for a kitchen and workshops, two granaries, and a barracks for soldiers stationed at the mission. San Ignacio (established 1728) still had an adobe church built during the Jesuit period. Work had begun on a larger stone structure, but had been suspended due to a lack of funds. Other structures included at least one granary, a barracks for soldiers stationed at the mission, a dormitory for single women and widows, and a *ranchería* of houses for Indian families most likely built of adobe that formed a square with two entrances. The final example is San Fernando (established 1769), the only Franciscan mission on the peninsula. The Franciscans had directed the construction of an adobe church and residence, a granary of the same material, and other smaller structures including a dovecote and chicken coop (figure 2.1).

The buildings erected by the Jesuits and Franciscans reflected the nature of the mission program. The large Indian populations, particularly at the older missions established in the central sections of the peninsula, were not fully integrated into what might be called a system. Because of the limitations of food production at the peninsula missions most converts continued to reside in rancherías and supported themselves through food collection and hunting. Converts periodically came to the mission to receive instruction from the missionaries in order to supplement what catechists who resided in the rancherías taught. Since the missionaries did not exercise much oversight over baptized Indians, social control was not a serious concern. The evidence from the Jesuit and Franciscan periods shows that the complexes consisted of the church, residence for the missionaries, granaries, workshops, and housing for the Indians. Dormitories, especially for single women and widows, did exist but were not a general part of mission policy.

Indian policy in the peninsula missions changed under the Dominicans, and the changes reflected conditions unique to the peninsula

BUILDING THE MISSIONS 41

Figure 2.1 **Plan of San Fernando Mission Located in Northern Baja California**

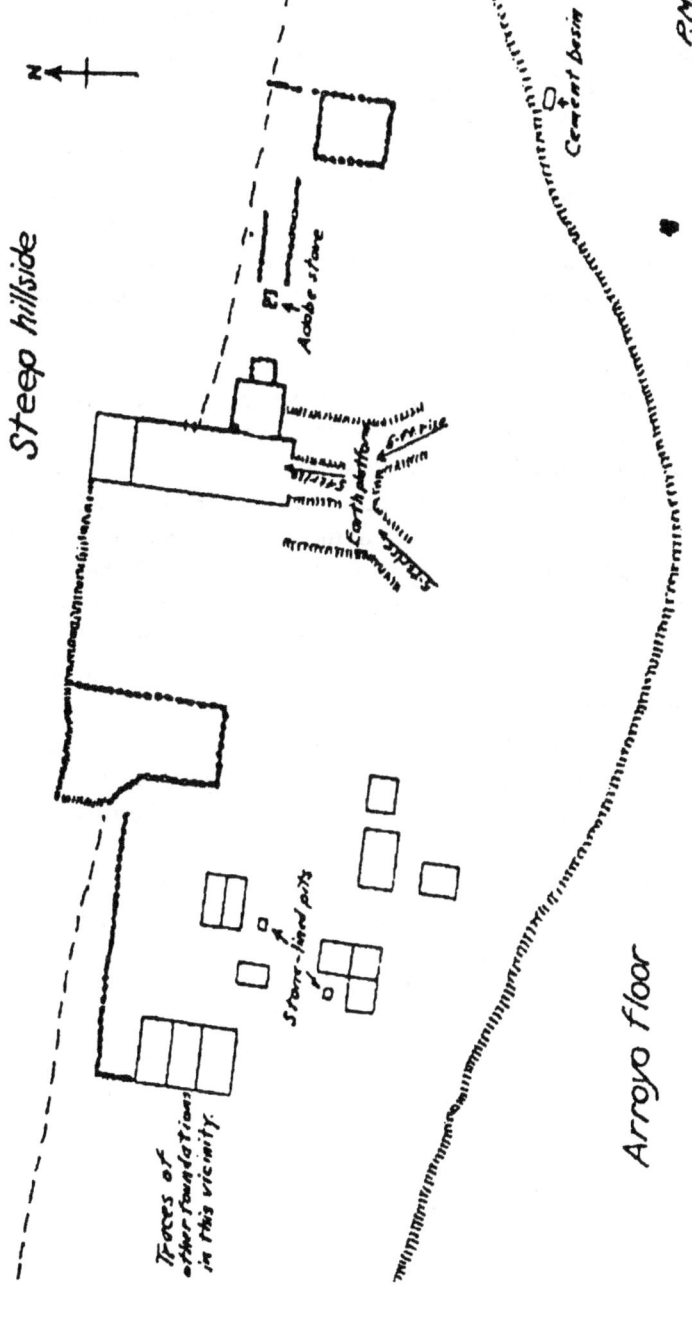

Source: Carl Sauer and Peveril Meigs, "Site and Culture at San Fernando de Velicatá," *University of California Publications in Geography* 2(9), 271–203 (1927).

as well as a shift in royal policy with the initiation of the so-called Bourbon Reforms. The Jesuit expulsion in 1768 and the organization in the peninsula of the colonization of Alta California beginning in 1769 led to the movement of more people between Baja California and the mainland and the rapid spread of disease through the peninsula missions. The Indian populations living in the missions dropped precipitously after 1768, and especially between 1768 and 1782 when a series of severe epidemics killed several thousand Indians. The Dominican establishments on the northern Pacific coast of the peninsula also had smaller populations than the missions further south, and the Dominicans imposed greater control over the available labor force.

The colonial reforms of the late eighteenth century placed a greater emphasis not only on the self-sufficiency of the missions, but where possible also on employing indigenous labor to help defray the costs of colonization of the frontier, as was the case in Alta California. In the missions of northwestern New Spain the changed colonial philosophy also led to greater social control in the missions, which included more of an emphasis on establishing stronger moral codes for behavior, especially of unmarried women. Dormitories for single women became a more common feature of mission building complexes in the peninsula missions. By the 1790s dormitories for women were among the first structures erected.

The Dominicans built the new frontier missions of adobe. A more complete record survives of the building projects at the Dominican missions. The first example is Rosario, which was the first Dominican mission, established in 1774 (figure 2.2, table 2.1). In 1793, the adobe church measured 46 x 9 varas, and from 1794 to 1800 the Dominicans directed the construction of a number of buildings. The new structures included infirmaries for men and women, a forge, and a wing of apartments for indigenous families erected in 1795; a dispensary built in 1798; and two buildings constructed in 1799 at Rancho San José including an adobe structure that may have been a chapel and an oratorio. In the following year a storeroom, kitchen, weaving room, and forge were built. In about 1802 the spring at Rosario failed, and the Dominicans moved the mission to a new site that most likely was Rancho San José. Ruins exist today at both mission sites, and the latter site is considerably smaller than the complex at the former. However, the move to a new location did not necessarily signify the complete abandonment of the older buildings.

Figure 2.2 **Plan of Rosario Mission Located in Northern Baja California**

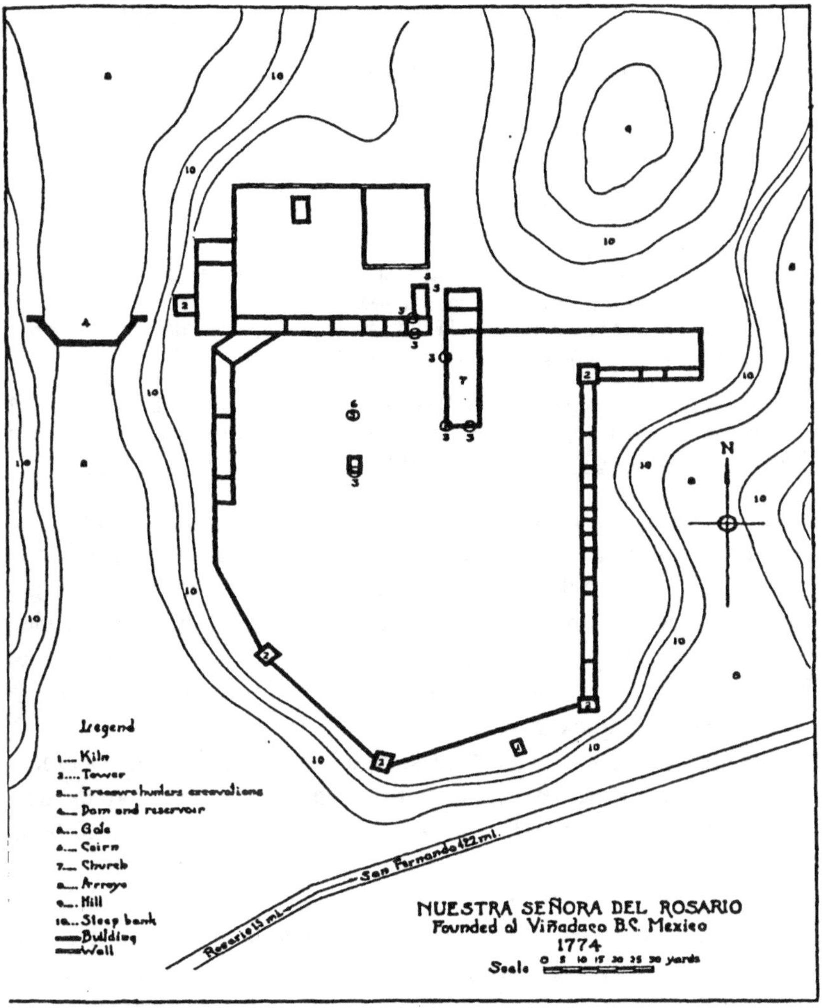

Source: Peveril Meigs, *The Dominican Mission Frontier of Lower California*. Berkeley: University of California Press, 1935.

The second case study is Santo Domingo mission, established in 1775. In 1793 the church was a structure built of adobe and poles measuring 18 x 8 varas. The missionaries reported considerable building activity in the late 1790s. In 1795 the church was rebuilt and expanded and the walls on other buildings were raised. Moreover, the Dominicans directed

Table 2.1

Building Construction Reported at Rosario Mission, 1794–1800

1793:	The church was an adobe structure with dimensions of 46 x 9 varas.
1794:	A new cemetery opened.
1795:	Two infirmaries built, one for men and the other for women. Other structures built included a forge and a wing of habitations for Indian converts.
1796:	Existing buildings repaired, and a corral built.
1797:	Existing buildings repaired and reroofed.
1798:	A dispensary 8 varas long built.
1799:	An adobe structure and oratory built at Rancho San José. The mission was moved to San José about three years later.
1800:	Four adobe structures built including a storeroom that measured 12 x 6 varas, a kitchen, forge, and weaving room.

Sources: Annual Reports, Archivo General de la Nación, Mexico, D.F., Misiones 2 and Provincias Internas 19; Zephyrin Engelhardt, O.F.M., *Missions and Missionaries of California: Lower California*, 2d edition (Mission Santa Barbara, 1929), 613–614.

the development of a farming outpost at San Telmo in a valley to the north of the mission that included a chapel, residence for the missionaries when they visited the site, quarters for the Indian workers, a granary, and other structures. In 1799 development of San Telmo apparently ended with the completion of an irrigation system. The Dominicans also put the native converts to work developing a new irrigation system at the main mission complex in 1797.

The final example is Santo Tomás, established in 1791. The documentary record reports the development of the mission complex from the date of establishment, and the relocation of the mission to a new site in 1794. In 1793, the chapel at the first site was an adobe structure that measured 12 x 5 varas. Following the relocation of the mission in 1794 the missionaries directed the construction of new buildings. Two churches were built, a temporary church in 1794 and a larger structure completed in 1801, a residence for the missionaries, a dormitory for older girls and single women and a second dormitory for single men, a dispensary, granary, storerooms, weaving room, and other structures. The growing Dominican concern for social control was reflected in the construction of dormitories. The first for girls and single women was completed in 1796, two years after the relocation of the mission to a new site. The dormitory for single men was completed in the same year. With a growing population of converts, the Dominicans ordered the building of a new and larger dormitory for girls and single women in 1801 (table 2.2).

Figure 2.3 **Plan of Santa Catalina Mission Located in Northern Baja California**

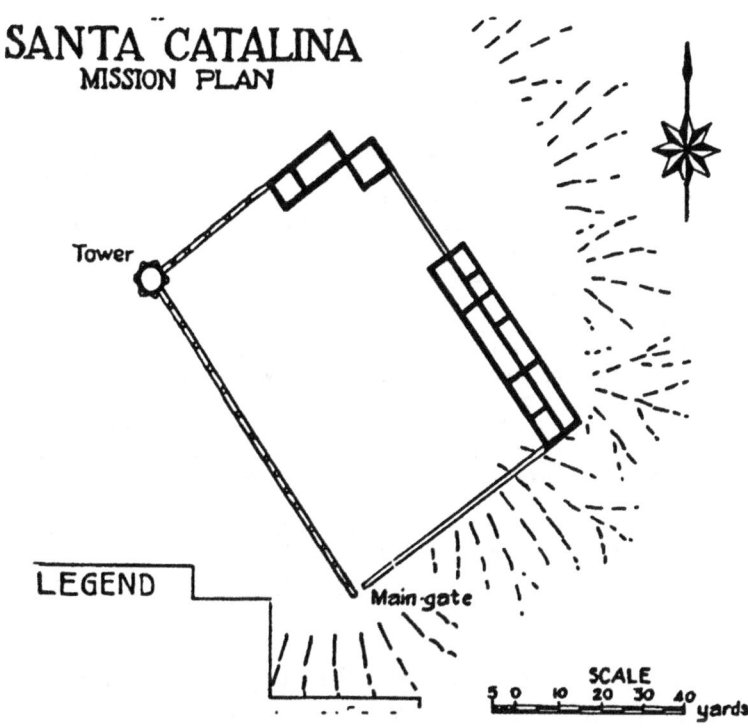

Source: Peveril Meigs, *The Dominican Mission Frontier of Lower California*. Berkeley: University of California Press, 1935.

The construction of dormitories also figured in the record of building at other Dominican missions. The Dominicans established Santa Catalina in 1797, and included dormitories for single women and girls in projects for 1797 and 1799 (figure 2.3). Other features suggest greater concern for social control, as well as defense. The northern Dominican mission building complexes were surrounded by walls, and may have had small bastions added to these walls. There are also references to small forts located close to several of the missions. The defensive configuration of the building complexes

Table 2.2

Building Construction Reported at Santo Tomás Mission, 1794–1801

1793:	Church described as being of adobe with dimensions of 12 x 5 varas.
1794:	Mission, originally established in 1791, was moved to a new site. An adobe chapel and residence for the missionaries were built.
1795:	Seventy varas of foundation laid for new buildings.
1796:	An adobe structure was built containing a reception room (sala), two bedrooms, another room, and a common area. A disepnsary was built, as well as dormitories for single men and single women. A weaving room with an adjoining corral was built.
1797:	A corral for sheep and goats was built. 1,400 varas of foundtion were laid for building projects.
1798:	No building projects reported, because indigenous workers prepared new argicultural fields.
1799:	Four adobe structures were built measuring 20, 14, 7, and 6 varas in length respectively. Foundations were laid for a new church.
1800:	Work continued on the church. A corridor, weaving room, and granary were built.
1801:	The adobe church begun in 1799 was completed. It measured 30 x 6 varas. Two store rooms, each measuring 10 x 8 varas, were built, as well as a new dormitory for single women and girls measuring 9 x 6 varas.

Sources: Annual Reports, Archivo General de la Nación, Mexico, D.F., Misiones 2 and Provincias Internas 19; Zephyrin Engelhardt, O.F.M., *Missions and Missionaries of California: Lower California*, 2d edition (Mission Santa Barbara, 1929), 625–626.

reflected both the instability of the northern Baja California frontier, and the greater concern for control of the indigenous population.

Concern for control of the indigenous populations also figured into the development of building complexes in Alta California. In the early period the Franciscans directed the construction of building complexes that in some instances contained defensive features. The San Diego, site of a major indigenous attack in 1775, was built for defense in the decade after the attack. A description of the buildings written in 1783 noted that the main buildings formed three wings of a square and a wall formed the fourth wall of the square, making the mission easily defensible. The complex also included barracks for the soldiers stationed at the mission, and the presence of a handful of soldiers was a standard practice at all of the missions. Other features enhanced social control, especially the building of dormitories for girls and single women and single men. An analysis of building chronologies shows that the Franciscans generally directed the construction of dormitories for girls and single women and perhaps men within the first years following the establishment of a mission. In

Figure 2.4 View (c. 1880) of the ruins of the first site of La Purísma Mission, showing the configuration of the main building complex.

Source: Noticias, *21: 1 (1957): 11*. Reproduced by permission of the Santa Barbara Historical Society.

Table 2.3

Building Construction Reported at La Purísima Mission, 1788–1835

1788:	Temporary structures of palisade or adobe with roofs of packed earth built, including a chapel, quarters for the missionaries, a granary, two rooms for which a use was not specified.
1789:	A church, granary, and common kitchen built of adobe.
1790:	A wing with seven rooms of adobe added to the growing complex, and a kiln built to fire roof tiles. After 1790 buildings constructed of adobe with tile roofs.
1791:	A granary of adobe built as a part of the main quadrangle, and three buildings erected outside of the quadrangle including a kitchen, oven, and chicken coop.
1792:	The adobe church and a granary renovated.
1793:	An adobe wing containing new quarters for the missionaries, apartments for visitors, and office, a storage room for Indian clothing, and a kitchen added to the main quadrangle.
1794:	A soldier's barracks, apartment for the mayordomo (overseer), a carpenter shop, and tack room built.
1795:	A granary and office built.
1796:	Three store rooms built.
1797:	A new residence built for the missionaries.
1798:	A new barracks with nine rooms built for the mission guard. The foundations for a larger church laid.
1799:	Two rooms built.
1800:	A wing with eight rooms added to the mission complex.
1802:	The adobe church begun in 1798 completed. A garden enclosed with an adobe wall.
1804:	A new barracks built for the mission guard.
1808:	A dam and aqueduct built.
1810:	A granary and house built at Rancho San Antonio north of the mission.
1812:	An earthquake and heavy rains in December of 1812 destroyed most of the mission complex. The report prepared at the end of 1812 noted that temporary buildings had been put up, and mentioned 100 housing units for Indian families not previously reported in the annual reports, as well as a dormitory for girls and single women.
1813:	In April of 1813 the mission moved to a new site several miles away. A temporary church built of palisade with an adobe veneer, and other temporary buildings erected.
1815:	A large adobe structure completed that contained quarters for the missionaries, apartments for visitors to the mission, a weaving room, and a chapel.
1816:	A large adobe structure built with quarters for the mission guard, quarters for the mayordomo, and workrooms. A hospital built.
1817:	Foundations laid for a new church, although there is no evidence that the larger church was ever completed. A fountain added to the Indian village.
1818:	The temporary church built in 1813 collapsed, and was replaced by a new temporary church built of adobe. The church completed in 1818 may have been built on the foundations laid in the previous year.
1821:	A bell tower added to the church.
1823:	More housing units added to the Indian village.
1835:	The chapel in the building constructed in 1815 renovated, because the church completed in 1818 was in poor condition. The renovated chapel served for the Indian population already reduced in size.

Sources: Zephyrin Engelhardt, O.F.M., *Mission La Purisima Concepcion de Mariá Santisima* (Santa Barbara, 1932); La Purísima Mission Annual Reports, Archivo General de la Nación, Mexico, D.F.; and the Santa Barbara Mission Archive–Library, Santa Barbara, California.

BUILDING THE MISSIONS   49

Figure 2.5 Diagram (c. 1818) Showing a Section of the Building Complex of Santa Clara Mission

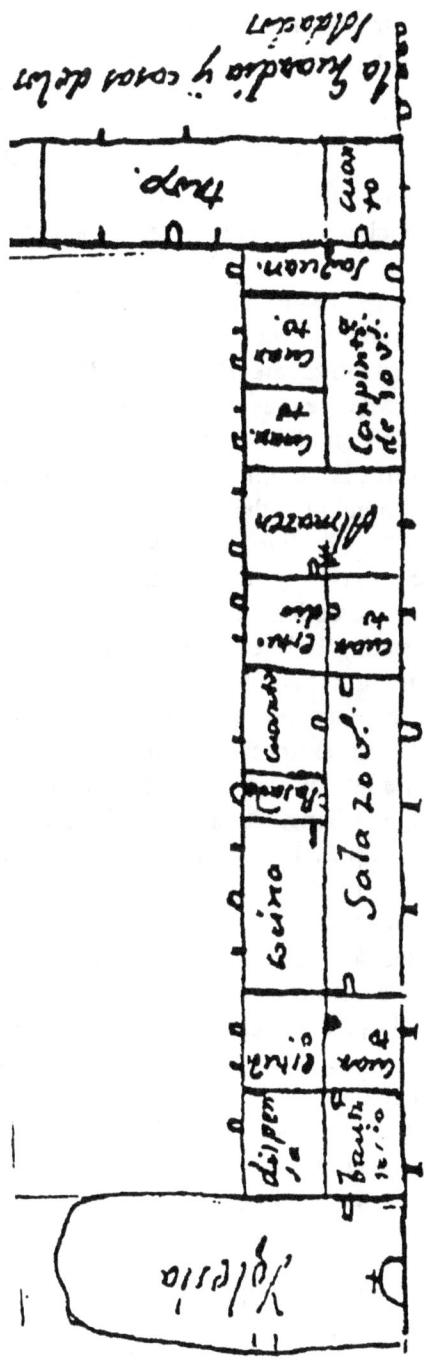

Source: Untitled account book for Santa Clara Mission, "Documentos Para la Historia de Mexico." Archivo General de Mexico, Mexico, D.F.

fifteen cases the first reference to dormitories was within five years of the establishment of a mission. Other forms of housing for the indigenous population also enhanced social control. The missionaries had permanent housing built for indigenous families. In some cases these were small apartments in much larger buildings, or else small single-family apartments. Evidence suggests that in some instances walls surrounded the native villages, which would have limited the ability of the natives to escape.

The mission building complexes in Alta California took 20 to 30 years to complete and generally were in the form of a quadrangle with structures also located outside of the main square. By the first decades of the nineteenth century the danger of indigenous attack on the missions was minimal, so defensive architecture similar to that of the Texas missions was not included in the California complexes. A case study of La Purísima, established in 1788, highlights the development of the mission complex (figure 2.4, table 2.3). La Purísima mission occupied two different sites for twenty-five and twenty-one years, respectively, and the Franciscans directed the construction of extensive building complexes at both sites. The devastating 1812 earthquake forced the abandonment of the site chosen for the mission in 1787 and relocation to a new site several miles away. There are several examples of the relocation of missions to new sites, but the shifts came within several years of establishment. For example, the Franciscans relocated San Diego, San Juan Capistrano, San Gabriel, and Santa Clara. Santa Clara offers the only other case of one of the California missions being relocated after the development of an extensive building complex, but the change involved only a short distance (figure 2.5).

Annual reports prepared by the Franciscans at the end of each year contain summaries of any building construction projects, including in some instances the dimensions as well as the building use. The reports describe the development of extensive and functional building complexes designed to form the core for self-sufficient towns. Churches stood as the largest and dominant structure, built on a scale to impress upon the Indians the grandeur of the new religion. The Franciscans had three churches built at the first mission site. The first was a temporary structure of palisade with a packed earth roof on beams erected in 1788. The temporary church was replaced in the following year with an adobe structure also with a packed earth roof. During the 1790s the number of Indians living at the mission increased, and the 1789 church was not large enough. In 1792, the

51

Figure 2.6 Photograph (c. 1880) of the Ruins of the First Site of La Purísima Mission, Lompoc, California

Reproduced by permission of the Santa Barbara Historical Society.

Figure 2.7 **Ruins of the First Site of La Purísima Mission, Lompoc, California.** The stone walls were a part of the front of the chuch, completed in 1802, and flanked the front entrance to the church. In the circa 1880 photograph of the ruins (figure 2.6), the church occupied the central part of the mission complex. The houses in the background occupy sections of the former mission complex.

Photograph by Robert H. Jackson.

Franciscans had the adobe church enlarged and added a tile roof. In 1798, the cornerstone was laid for a new and larger adobe church, completed in 1802 or 1803. This was the church destroyed in the 1812 earthquake.

The Franciscans directed the construction of a variety of other buildings at the first site. Residences for the missionaries had a top priority in building projects, and the record shows the construction of apartments for the Franciscans in 1788, 1793, and 1797. Granaries to store mission crops were an important part of the building complexes and appear in the record in 1788, 1791, and 1795. Additionally, the Franciscans had buildings erected at farms located at different spots within the mission territory. In 1810, a granary and residence were built at Rancho San Antonio to the north of the mission.

Other structures served to enhance social control at the mission. A permanent detachment of soldiers resided there both to protect the Franciscans and to control the Indian populations. Indian laborers built barracks for the mission guard in 1794, and a new and larger barracks in 1804. The Franciscans ordered the incarceration at night of single women and older girls in dormitories, and a dormitory had been built at La Purísima by 1802. They ordered the construction of dormitories from the beginning of the development of the missions. Ecclesiastical authorities later directed the construction of dormitories in Baja California and other frontier missions. There is evidence that the missionaries also had European-style housing for Indian families. The report on the damage to mission buildings caused by the 1812 earthquake included 100 small apartments for Indian families. The configuration of the Indian housing at the first site of La Purísima is not known, but evidence from several other missions including Santa Bárbara shows that in some instances walls enclosed Indian housing.

The 1812 annual report dated December 31 contained a description of the damage caused by the severe earthquake on December 21, 1812:

> Some of the workshops went down, but some more strongly built may serve as habitations if not for minor uses which require no such security. One hundred houses of neophyte Indians and the pozolera [community kitchen], the walls of which were an adobe and a half thick and roofed with tiles, have become inserviceable. The garden walls of adobe, covered with tiles, have either collapsed or threaten to fall.

Extensive ruins of the first mission complex survived into the early part of this century, but urban development has wiped out most of the ruins (see figures 2.6 and 2.7).

Three months later, in March of 1813, Friar Mariano Payeras, O.F.M., wrote to propose relocating the mission several miles north to a site known as Los Berros. Payeras also provided further details on the damage to the mission buildings at the first site:

Figure 2.8 **Reconstructed Buildings at the Second Site of La Purísima Mission, Lompoc, California**

Photograph by Robert H. Jackson.

> In view of what this promises we have examined the interior of the granaries, and we have observed with sorrow that all these structures are ruined from the foundations to the roof: that the church is demolished from the foundations up: and that neither Fathers, nor soldiers, nor neophytes will or can, without terror or risk, live in their habitations, which have partially fallen, are partly out of plomb, and all in many parts [are] seriously cracked.

The Franciscans moved the mission to Los Berros in April of the same year, and directed the construction of temporary buildings built of palisades with an adobe veneer. Over the next decade Payeras had a new complex of buildings constructed in an unusual configuration. Instead of a quadrangle as had been built at the first mission site and at most of the other missions, the new buildings were laid out along a line at the base of one of the hills that borders the Los Berros valley. In 1815, the church erected in 1813 was repaired, and a building with 21 rooms including a residence for the missionaries and a small private chapel for the use of the Franciscans was built. In the following year another long building containing quarters for the mission guard and mayordomo (overseer) and workshops was built (see figure 2.8).

In 1817, foundations were laid for a new permanent church that was never completed. In 1818, the temporary church built in 1813 collapsed and was replaced by another adobe structure that remained in use until the early 1830s. After abandoning plans to complete the church started in 1817, the Franciscans had a cemetery and bell tower added in 1821 to the church built in 1818. One wall of the 1818 church rested on a small spring, which so damaged the structure that it had to be abandoned around 1835. The chapel in the long building erected in 1815 was remodeled to serve as a temporary chapel, and was large enough for the Indian population already reduced in size to about 400.

Details on the construction of housing for the Indian population are incomplete. In 1816, a hospital was built for the Indian population, and older buildings were remodeled to provide additional hospital space. The 1817 report mentioned the Indian ranchería (village), but provided few details. The 1823 annual report mentioned the construction of ten residences for as many Indian families. In the late 1950s and early 1960s archaeological excavations identified two adjoining structures that consisted of small apartments for Indian families. The two structures measured 335 feet and 200 feet in length respectively.

Conclusions

Following the closing of the missions, many of the buildings deteriorated for lack of maintenance and/or because local settlers used the old structures as sources of building materials. Moreover, the missionaries and the indigenous populations often abandoned the missions and left them to decay. Toward the end of the nineteenth century Anglo Americans rediscovered what might be called the "mystique" of the missions and the Spanish heritage throughout the southwest. Groups such as the California Landmarks Club sought to preserve and restore the remaining mission structures. Most often it was the church that survived, and many other buildings lay in ruins or were razed to make room for streets and other improvements in towns that developed around a number of former missions. Scholars also began to explore the history of the missions and the experiences of the native peoples congregated on them, State and federal governments also converted a number of mission sites into historical landmarks that are visited today by thousands of tourists. Thus, architectural legacy of the missions survives, although it is often misinterpreted.

Chapter 3

Social and Cultural Change

The mission program envisioned a radical transformation in the culture, religion and worldview, and social structure and social relations of the indigenous population. The Franciscan, Jesuit, and Dominican missionaries congregated indigenous peoples from diverse cultures and lifeways, which meant that the program of change developed in different ways in the various frontier jurisdictions. The natives of New Mexico were sedentary agriculturalists living in stratified and hierarchical communities. The natives of northern Sonora were also sedentary agriculturalists, but practiced a pattern of seasonal migration to exploit certain sources of wild foods, including cactus fruit, during the period following the harvest of crops. The descriptions of native society in the mid- and late seventeenth century depict conditions following at least a century of disease to epidemics that spread along established trade routes from central Mexico. Some scholars have argued that disease radically transformed native society in Sonora prior to the establishment of missions, and caused the collapse of more sophisticated systems of government and the dispersal of nucleated settlements into *rancherias* with family compounds located at greater distances from each other. The indigenous populations of Baja California and central Texas were largely nomadic hunters and gatherers who hunted and collected plant and other types of food within clearly defined territories.

Texas historically had a variety of native cultures. The Hasinais (Caddo) of eastern Texas were sedentary agriculturalists organized into a sophisticated tribal confederation. Located on the border of Spanish and French influence, the Hasinais evidenced extreme ambivalence toward the Spanish mission program. The Orcoquisac, a sedentary group closely related to the Hasinais, also received the mission program in a lukewarm fashion. To the north and west the groups identified by the Spanish as Apaches and Comanches competed for control of the buffalo hunting grounds on the southern plains, and the warrior-hunters completely rejected the notion of sedentary life. The Franciscan missionaries achieved the greatest level of success among the nomadic hunter-gatherer bands from northern Mexico and Texas known today as Coahuiltecans, but the primary motivation for the Coahuiltecans to enter the missions included finding greater subsistence security as well as trying to find allies against the plains bands that raided the Coahuiltecans. The final group in Texas to mention is the Karankawas, bands of hunters and gatherers that lived along the lower gulf coast. The Karankawas bands migrated on a seasonal basis between permanent village sites along the coast and creeks in the interior within about ten miles of the coast, exploiting different food resources. Along the coast the Karankawas fished and collected shellfish, while in the interior they hunted and collected wild plant foods. Unlike the Coahuiltecans, the Karankawas bands generally did not settle on the missions, and the Franciscans constantly complained that the military did not do enough to force the Indians to remain at the missions.

Baja California, a largely inhospitable desert peninsula, supported a sparse population of hunters and gatherers that lived in small bands. Water was the key to survival, and one strategy used by the Jesuit and later Franciscan and Dominican missionaries was to take control of the sources of water. The Spanish used different pseudoethnic terms to describe the native peoples of the peninsula, but there were few differences in terms of social and economic organization and the ways that the missionaries attempted to deal with incorporating the native peoples into the missions. The one modification the missionaries made was to allow a large part of the indigenous population to continue to reside in numerous settlement sites known as rancherías. The agriculture introduced by the Jesuits produced only enough to feed a segment of the population, so the Jesuits had to allow the bulk of the natives to continue to support themselves through traditional hunting and collection of plant and other foods. Periodically the converts living in the rancherías spent time at the main mission village (*cabecera*) to receive religious indoctrination. This pattern limited the effectiveness of the mission program of directed social-cultural change and evangelization, and allowed shaman to continue to influence the natives. Earlier Jesuit reports complained about the continued influence of shamans, but as long as a sizable population continued to reside outside of the day-to-day control of the missionaries the persistence of traditional religion was a problem. It was only with the decline in the indigenous population that the missionaries were able to congregate most and finally all of the converts at the mission cabecera.

The region known as Alta California provided a much richer food base, and in particular the abundance of acorns made conventional agriculture unnecessary. California's environment supported one of the highest population densities, and sophisticated societies flourished, especially along the coast. The economy relied on collection and processing of acorns and other wild plant foods supplemented by hunting and fishing and the collection of marine foods. The Chumash, perhaps the most advanced society in pre-Hispanic California, supported craft specialists and religious specialists. Political authority rested in village chiefs, who could be either male or female. As was the case with other groups in California, the Chumash traded extensively to acquire a greater variety of foods and raw materials, and also sought marriage partners outside of the village. Political, economic, and social ties between villages were important if not vital for survival, and the Spanish mission program seriously disrupted the links between communities.

This chapter will examine selected aspects of cultural change in the missions. Because the information from the different regions of northern Mexico varies in terms of completeness, I will present selected examples that illustrate major points that I am making. The first topic is the limits of evangelization.

The Limits of Evangelization

Religion was one of the elements that defined the status of colonial peoples in Spanish America. The subjects of the king were to be at least nominally Catholic. Religious conversion was a major element in Spanish Indian policy, and priests working in conjunction with civil officials attempted to stamp out pre-Hispanic practices and religious leaders. The mission evangelization program targeted two distinct groups of Indians: adults and young children. The basic assumption of the missionaries was that adults generally would acquire only a veneer of Christianity at best; the religious education of young children received greater attention, and in the long run the missionaries believed that they would achieve a higher degree of success in creating a fundamentally Catholic indigenous population. Active resettlement of Indians to the missions complicated the process of religious indoctrination, since the mission populations would consist of individuals with varying degrees of knowledge of the basic doctrine, rituals, and prayers taught to the converts. The mix of recent converts, older converts, and children raised at the missions included many individuals who were Catholic only in name and may have secretly continued to practice traditional rituals. The persistence of traditional religious practices in the mission communities made it difficult for the missionaries to shield converts, particularly young children, from what they saw as the corrosive influence of shamanism.

Language was one barrier to effective evangelization, and religious indoctrination was rendered even more difficult because of the imprecision of translating culturally embedded concepts to the indigenous languages that in many instances did not have similar concepts. A good example of this problem is recorded in Francisco Clavigero's *History of California*. Clavigero recorded how Jesuit missionary Eusebio Kino attempted to explain the death and resurrection of Christ to a group of Cochimies in Baja California in the mid-1680s. Kino placed some flies in cold water to stun them, and then placed the flies in the sun. The warmth of the sun revived the flies. The missionary recorded what the Cochimies said, but, as a later Jesuit fluent in Cochimies's language pointed out, Kino misinterpreted the reaction of the Indians to the revival of the flies. The Cochimies reportedly said "*Ibi-muhuet-e-tedommo, gaijenji juajib omui*," which translates to "although it has been stunned a little while, it arose suddenly." The understanding of the resurrection was not adequately conveyed to the Cochimies.

Missionaries who spent many years at a single mission or in missions inhabited by converts speaking the same language or similar dialects gained with the passage of time high levels of fluency in the indigenous languages, and could in some cases even preach in them. However, many missionaries remained at a mission for only a short period of time, and when assigned to a new station had to begin to learn a new language. This could work to the benefit of traditional religious leaders, since the basic elements of indigenous beliefs often remained a mystery to the missionaries. This also meant that those missionaries with a good command of indigenous language could and often did probe deeply to uncover the nature of religious practices. The limited language skills of missionaries is highlighted by a report on the Pimería Alta missions of northern Sonora prepared in 1764 by Manuel Aguirre, S.J. According to Aguirre, the Pimas living on the missions recited their prayers in their own language. Moreover, Aguirre noted that the missionaries stationed in the missions had varying levels of proficiency in the Pimas language, but doubted that any of the missionaries could preach in Pimas. The Jesuits used interpreters, and also attempted to teach the Pimas Spanish.

Language could be a double-edged sword, as seen in instances of missionaries stationed at a single mission community over a long period of time. The 1824 Chumash uprising in Alta California resulted, in part, from the use of new confessional aids written in the native language by several Franciscan missionaries who already had a detailed knowledge of Chumash language and culture. The Franciscans designed the confessional aids to root out surviving religious practices as well as social-cultural practices such as incestuous sexual relations between siblings. The uprising occurred shortly before Easter, which was one of the periods when the missionaries required indigenous converts to confess. On the other hand, many of the Franciscans stationed in California had little or no understanding of the basic elements of native religious beliefs. In 1813, for example, the Spanish *cortes* (parliament) sent a detailed questionnaire to be answered by the Franciscans stationed in the California missions. The responses varied, but it was also very clear that many of the Franciscans had little or no understanding of indigenous religion. Language certainly aided the natives in erecting a shield against the Franciscans probing too deeply into their traditional religious beliefs.

The way that the missionaries measured the success of their evangelization contributed to the ability of some native converts to hold on to their traditional beliefs. The missionaries measured the success of the evangelization programs in the numbers of Indians confessing, receiving communion, and reciting prayers learned through rote memorization. Baptism initiated a convert into the Christian community, and confession and communion marked passages to a level of basic understanding of Catholic doctrine. Baptism also marked passage into the categories used to differentiate between those within and those outside Spanish colonial society. At first, progress toward achieving the goal of preparing baptized Indians for the basic sacraments was slow. In 1720, for example, Jesuit Julián de Mayorga stationed at San José de Comondú in Baja California noted that few Indian converts received communion. Further, he wrote that adults still adhered to traditional religious practices. Reports written by Jesuit missionaries in 1744 commented on the progress of evangelization. Joseph Gasteiger, stationed at Guadalupe in Baja California, reported progress in the evangelization of the Indians: all adults confessed yearly, while some received communion. Clemente Guillán, stationed at Dolores also in Baja California, shared this optimistic tone. He reported progress in evangelization despite having to overcome obstacles that included language, since he had to preach through interpreters while at the same time teaching the Indians Spanish and having to challenge the influence of traditional religious leaders. At San Francisco Xavier, Miguel del Barco reported that the Indians knew doctrine well. Most confessed yearly and many received communion. In a report drafted eighteen years later, in 1762, del Barco noted that he believed that no shaman remained, and the majority of Indians living at the mission had been baptized as young children and fulfilled obligations such as confession and communion in large numbers.

Reports from the Pimería Alta presented, in some instances, a different picture of the progress of the Jesuit evangelization program. The evangelization of the northern Pimas proved to be far more complex than in Baja California. The Jesuits and later the Franciscans congregated new Pimas converts to the missions throughout the entire period, and during the Jesuit period a number of missions did not have resident missionaries for extended periods of time, and the veneer of Christianity was extremely thin at best. The 1744 report for San Francisco Xavier del Bac mission written by Joseph de Torres Perea highlights the limited impact of evangelization in mission communities that had received minimal attention. Torres Perea reported that the administration of the sacrament of baptism had not transformed the Indians, and most converts had not even learned basic prayers. Moreover, most marriages were celebrated according to traditional practices. The first Franciscans to replace the Jesuits in the Pimería Alta echoed Torres Perea's opinion of the course of evangelization. Juan Joseph Agorreta, stationed at Saric, commented that the Pimas were "little more than gentiles," and that few had received communion. Juan Díaz, O.F.M., at Caborca, noted that the Indians living in the missions lacked discipline and, because of the shortage of missionaries during the Jesuit period, had been inadequately instructed in Catholic doctrine and theology.

A degree of religious syncretism (the blending of religious traditions) also occurred as a result of the mission evangelization programs in northern Mexico. New Mexico offers an intriguing example of syncretism.

During the seventeenth century Franciscan missionaries engaged in repression of traditional religion, and publicly punished traditional religious leaders who kept the old beliefs alive underground. Religious repression was one factor contributing to the great revolt of 1680, which expelled the Spaniards for twelve years. Following the Spanish reconquest of New Mexico in the 1690s and the suppression of the last spasms of indigenous resistance, the Franciscans adopted a policy of appeasement towards the natives. The new approach resulted in the abandonment of the more rigorous effort to root out traditional religious practices, and more tolerance for dances and other rites. The syncretism can best be seen in the survival today of the *Katchina* (the rain gods that brought life to the crops) and the *Matachines* dance (depicting Christians versus Moors). Missionaries in central Mexico used religious plays and pageantry as tools in conversion. Mass spectacles attracted the imagination of converts, and provided public rituals that replaced the pre-Hispanic ones the missionaries sought to exterminate. The Franciscans employed similar strategies in converting the natives of New Mexico.

A second example of syncretism comes from Alta California. Following the 1824 Chumash uprising, a large group of some 400 converts fled from Santa Bárbara missions to a site in the lower San Joaquín Valley. At this site the Chumash created a community based on an economy that combined Spanish agriculture and animal husbandry with traditional hunting and collection of wild plant foods. Moreover, the Chumash practiced a syncretic religion that blended traditional practices along with the adoration of the Christian cross. The religious leaders of the community maintained an altar with vessels taken from the mission, along with the cross that stood at the center of the new religion. The Chumash community survived for more than a decade, but was wiped out in the late 1830s by a severe epidemic.

Religion was only one element of the program of directed cultural change on the missions, and the missionaries attempted to transform social relations and morals, gender labor roles, and even the use of clothing. Aspects of the campaign to change native society and culture reflected similar policies in central Mexico. The use of clothing by adults was one example of a policy first introduced in central Mexico that the missionaries also incorporated into their own program. During the mid- and late eighteenth century royal officials sought to encourage the indigenous population of central Mexico to dress more in line with Spanish notions of decency. The imperative to clothe the Indians also figured prominently in the frontier mission communities. However, changing clothing patterns was but one element of a larger effort to transform the indigenous way of life.

Aspects of Social Change in the Missions

From the outset of the establishment of the missions, the missionaries sought to modify or to eliminate certain social practices and to restructure indigenous society to conform more closely to their own notions of the standards that should be followed in sedentary Christian communities. At times the missionaries faced considerable difficulty in achieving these goals. Several Jesuits in the Pimería Alta remarked on the resistance of the Pimas to adopting a completely sedentary lifestyle, which entailed abandonment of seasonal transhumance from their fields to sources of wild plant food such as cactus fruit. In 1744, Joseph de Torres Perea noted that the Indians at San Francisco Xavier del Bac were still not used to living at the missions. Twenty years later the Jesuit assigned to the same mission reported that the pattern of seasonal transhumance persisted, but that the Pimas had to become completely sedentary if they were to become good Christians.

Missionaries in other regions of northern Mexico experienced similar problems. In Texas, for example, the Franciscans experienced difficulty in trying to force the Karankawas to settle permanently on the missions and break the pattern of seasonal transhumance. The Karankawas left and returned to the missions, and often returned to have children who had been born between visits baptized. The natives most likely viewed the missions as another seasonal source of food. The Franciscans constantly complained about the inability of the military to force the Karankawas to remain on the missions. Other native groups in Texas also refused to settle permanently on the missions. In the 1750s and 1760s the Franciscans operated missions for Lipan Apache bands, but the Apaches never settled for more than a short period of time. It appears that the band chiefs were more interested in securing Spanish military aid against the Comanches, a group that competed with the Apaches for control of the buffalo herds on the southern Great Plains. Once congregated on the missions, converts also fled to return either seasonally or permanently to areas beyond Spanish influence. This occurred in all of the frontier missions, and fugitives commonly sought refuge among groups hostile to the Spanish or at least still independent of Spanish control.

A recurring problem was the survival of those elements of traditional indigenous religious practices that the missionaries deemed unacceptable. The missionaries targeted traditional religious leaders in their campaigns to eliminate indigenous religion. Clemente Guillén, S.J., at Dolores mission in Baja California wrote in 1744 that he had burned the wooden tablets and other paraphernalia of the shaman. The Dominican Luis Sales described encounters with shamans, and also his efforts to stop dancing that the missionaries normally associated with Indian pagan beliefs. As noted above, Joseph de Torres Perea's report on the del Bac mission in the Pimería Alta in 1744 noted the survival of traditional practices such as marriage ceremonies, and indirect evidence of the presence of Pimas shamans who may have convinced many adults not to accept baptism, perhaps by associating the sacrament with high death rates during the frequent epidemics in the region.

The missionaries in both regions also attempted to eliminate other native social practices. For example, missionary Guillén also noted in his 1744 report that he had stamped out polygamy and infanticide: the Guaycurans killed the first-born child. In the Pimería Alta the missionaries had to deal with the use of *toloache* (datura), a drug that caused hallucinations that connected the individual to the spirit world, and in some cases caused death. Ignacio Pfefferkorn recorded several deaths caused by toloache at Guevavi mission, and then wrote about the use of the drug in his general description of Sonora.

In reshaping native society the missionaries attempted to impose European Christian standards of morality and decency. Unlike the corporate indigenous communities that enjoyed internal autonomy as long as they complied with the demands of the colonial state, the missionaries controlled or attempted to control most aspects of the day-to-day lives of the indigenous populations living on the missions. The effort to get the Indians to use European-style clothing is an example of the difficulties the missionaries faced in trying to get the neophytes to live by the new standards of conduct that distinguished them from non-Christians. The missionaries expended considerable resources to buy cloth for European-style clothes and to hire skilled weavers to teach converts how to produce cloth from locally grown cotton or wool from mission herds. The drive to clothe the indigenous population was a policy throughout Spanish America in the late colonial period, as Spanish officials pressured indigenous men and women to dress in conformity with European standards of decency. Several Jesuit missionaries in Baja California commented on their preoccupation with clothing the converts. One anonymous account noted, "The same thing applies to clothing since from their infertile homeland they did not even obtain a thread from which to cover themselves. Since it is absolutely necessary that the Indians wear some clothing when they come to church, and during their frequent and serious illness. . . ."

Wenceslao Linck, stationed at San Francisco de Borja, complained that "The mere statistics will enable you to understand what a difficult task I have in securing sufficient clothing for those naked savages."

Clothing for Indian converts figured into the costs of supporting the Baja and Alta California missions following the expulsion of the Jesuits. For example, an accounting of government funds expended on the missions in the Californias prepared on September 5, 1772, recorded the following expenditures: stipends for missionaries, 10,500 pesos; funds for supplies for Indians at recently established missions, 2,000 pesos; and the budget for clothing for the Indians, 4,000 pesos. This amounted to 24 percent of the funds set aside for the missions for one year.

Surviving account books from Texas and California missions record the importation of different types of cloth to be used for different purposes, including clothing the natives. Records from California missions also note the sale of cloth both imported and locally produced, to the military garrisons and settlers. Reports from the California missions also make references to textile production.

Shifts in Material Culture

Cultural change can also be measured through an analysis of material culture. However, there are relatively few archaeological studies that examine the material culture of the indigenous population living on the missions. One important study does offer a comparison of shifts in material culture at three California missions: San Antonio (1771); La Purísima (1788); Soledad (1791). The results of the analysis are suggestive of patterns at missions in other regions of northern Mexico.

The Franciscans stationed at Soledad mission actively congregated new converts during two phases: in the 1790s and first years of the nineteenth century; and again around 1820. During the years of congregation when the Franciscans brought many natives to live on the mission, the material assemblages continued to reflect the dominant survival of traditional material culture. On the other hand, in the years when congregation lagged and the population experienced a decline in numbers, the presence of traditional material culture actually declined and was replaced by introduced items. Therefore, the pace of congregation dictated the survival of material culture. The second finding has to do with the survival of material culture and the size of the indigenous populations living on the missions. The larger the indigenous population, the greater the retention of traditional material culture. The retention of traditional material culture was greatest at San Antonio and La Purísima missions, which in 1805 had maximum recorded populations of 1,296 and 1,520 respectively. Soledad, with a smaller maximum population of 688 (1805), evidenced the survival of less traditional material culture when compared to the two larger mission communities.

Population size and the pace of congregation modified the retention or loss of traditional material culture. The larger the concentration of Indian peoples, the greater the retention of culture. This conclusion has larger implications for other aspects of cultural change, especially religion. It supports the hypothesis that the larger the number of recent converts the greater the survival of traditional religious beliefs and syncretism.

Conclusions

The task of reshaping the fundamental way in which the native peoples viewed the cosmos and their place within the universe proved to be difficult at best for the missionaries. Equally difficult was the campaign to radically change every aspect of native life from religion to social relations, concepts of labor, and marriage practices. The evidence of the changes that did occur is biased, since it comes primarily from the perspective of the missionaries and/or civil and military officials. However, through the lens of the colonizers one can catch glimpses of native responses, consisting of both resistance and acquiescence to change. In many areas, such as religious beliefs, many natives accepted what the Spanish had to offer on their own terms, although often covertly. The evidence also suggests that mass religious conversion of indigenous populations in northern Mexico did not necessarily work as the missionaries had envisioned.

Chapter 4

Indigenous Resistance and Social Control

The "spiritual conquest" of the indigenous populations and the creation of a colonial order in northern New Spain was anything but peaceful, and the missionaries encountered resistance at all stages of the colonization process. This chapter examines patterns of Indian resistance to the creation of the Spanish colonial order. Resistance occurred because the native groups on the northern frontier attempted to retain their preconquest culture, social organization, religion, and worldview in the face of efforts made by the missionaries to reshape indigenous identity to conform to Spanish *indio* status. Resistance reveals how indigenous peoples felt violated by the imposition of Spanish cultural and religious norms. It represented a fracture line with the new hegemonic Spanish colonial society and culture and its norms on one side and the natives clinging to their lifeways on the other. Friction that at times turned violent separated the two.

This chapter outlines patterns of resistance along the fracture line of Spanish colonialism, and the ways in which patterns of resistance led to the creation by Spanish officials of pseudoethnic categories. It focuses on the cases of primary and secondary resistance in New Mexico culminating in the massive revolt that freed the region from Spanish domination for twelve years. The case of Baja California follows, where most resistance, both active and passive, originated with the Indians being brought under the control of the mission system. It is followed by a discussion of the Pimería Alta, a region that witnessed resistance by northern Pimas under varying degrees of control of the missionaries. There was also conflict with groups such as Apache bands and Seris, who raided the missions, pueblos, and ranches, and lived on the fringes of Spanish-controlled territory. Patterns of warfare contributed to the creation of pseudoethnic identities, since the Spanish tried to place larger collective labels on the different bands that raided the frontier. The terms Apache and Seri are examples of pseudoethnic labels that attempted to insinuate a larger common identity and political organization on culturally and linguistically related peoples. In northern Sonora, during the early phase of implementation of the mission program, Spaniards also created pseudoethnic categories to distinguish between friendly and potentially hostile Pimas living on the permanent streams in the region. The final examples are drawn from Texas and Alta California.

The analysis presented here is based on an examination of two forms of resistance: active and passive. Active resistance consisted of violent reactions to the Spanish colonial program, such as rebellion or the murder of missionaries. Passive resistance, generally more difficult to document, included a variety of expressions of discontent including flight, destruction of mission property, or work slowdowns. Resistance generally occurs in two stages: primary and secondary. Primary resistance was the initial violent response to the arrival of the missionaries, soldiers, and settlers, and their agenda for the change of native society. Traditional political leaders and shamans led the first opposition to the colonizers, and, in the case of Baja California, the missionaries first attempted to destroy the influence of shamans through a variety of means. Secondary resistance occurred after converts had lived for some time under the mission regime.

Indigenous Resistance in New Mexico

The history of Spanish-Pueblo relations, particularly in the sixteenth and seventeenth centuries, was characterized by violence and exploitation. The first Spanish expedition to the region lead by Francisco de Coronado in 1540–1542 was a disaster for the Pueblo peoples. For two years Coronado and his men conquered and exploited the Pueblos in a fruitless search for wealth characteristic of the extremely ruthless first generation of conquistadors. Coronado only abandoned New Mexico after a failed search for the fabled seven cities of Cibola and Gran Quivira, mythic societies reputed to be rich in gold, silver, and jewels. The Spaniards left behind communities scarred by Coronado's failed venture.

The *adelantado* Juan de Oñate's occupation of New Mexico, a privately funded venture also characteristic of the conquistador ruthlessness, also resulted in violent resistance, a residue of the earlier experience of Coronado's incursion there. In December of 1598, the Acomas rebelled against Oñate's new colonial order, killing his nephew Juan de Zaldívar and fifteen other Spaniards. Oñate's revenge was swift and brutal. Acoma warriors resisted until overwhelmed by the Spaniards. Many were put to death, and Oñate ordered the enslavement of 500 and the mutilation of some of the survivors. Oñate's brutal treatment of the Acomas was one of the reasons for his removal from power in 1607 by order of the king. However, the first eighty years of Spanish rule in New Mexico were based on the exploitation of the Pueblos as a conquered people, much like the Nahuatl speakers of central Mexico.

The Pueblo uprising of 1680 was the most serious challenge to Spanish rule in New Mexico. A number of factors contributed to the uprising. The Spanish settlers and the Franciscan missionaries made considerable demands on the Pueblos for labor and goods, especially corn and textiles. Civil and religious officials also fought over the spoils of native labor. At the same time, relations with neighboring indigenous peoples deteriorated, and groups such as the Apaches raided the Pueblos following the establishment of Spanish rule, especially in drought years when food on the Staked Plains was scarce. Moreover, food shortages and epidemics undermined the very fabric of native society and made it more difficult for the natives to comply with the demands of the settlers and missionaries. Finally, the Franciscans attempted to systematically exterminate all aspects of the Indian religion, and they persecuted the traditional Pueblo leaders—the war chiefs and war captains—who were responsible for protecting their religion. The missionaries also had the kivas filled with sand, and they persecuted Pope, a practioner of the old beliefs who would become one of the best known of the leaders of the rebellion.

The uprising began on August 10, 1680, and over the next several weeks the Indians killed 21 of the 33 Franciscans stationed in the province and about 400 settlers. The surviving settlers escaped a siege of Santa Fe, and withdrew to the area of modern El Paso. A count made in El Paso showed that slightly fewer than 2,000 people had survived the exodus from New Mexico. The Pueblos retained their independence for twelve years, but were once again conquered between 1692 and 1696 by Diego de Vargas. Squabbles between the individual Pueblos had shattered the unity that facilitated the uprising, and drought and raids by hostile Apache bands had reached a crisis level by the early 1690s. Only one group, the Hopi in eastern Arizona, never accepted missionaries again and retained their independence from the Spaniards. The 1680 revolt was the last major instance of Pueblo resistance, but the Spaniards and the Franciscans also realized that they could not return to the exploitative prerebellion economic system. The missionaries also were not as zealous in persecuting traditional Pueblo leaders, and allowed a degree of religious syncretism. During the eighteenth century a new balance returned to Spanish-Pueblo relations, and the major threat came from raids by Apaches, Comanches, and other groups living on the margins of New Mexico.

A sense of the native motives for rebellion comes from a handful of interrogations of Indians captured by the Spaniards before their exodus from New Mexico, or individuals who joined the Spaniards as they left New Mexico. Governor Antonio de Otermín interrogated one such individual named Pedro García on August 25, 1680. Identified as a Tagano from Las Salinas, Pedro García reported what he had been told by Bartolomé, the head *cantor* (singer) of Galisteo. Bartolomé had confronted the rebels coming to that pueblo, and had been told that the rebels "were tired of the work they had to do for the Spaniards and the religious, because they did not allow them [the Indians] to plant or do other things or do other things for their own needs[.]"

Resistance and Social Control in Baja California

From the arrival of the Jesuit missionaries at Loreto in Baja California, Indians resisted. In the weeks following the establishment of Loreto, Indians reportedly from four nearby rancherías attacked the mission. According to one source, as many as 500 Indian warriors were involved in the attack, and it was only the possession of firearms that tipped the balance in favor of the colonizers. As the mission frontier expanded in the peninsula the missionaries continued to encounter resistance, often from groups still unaffected by the mission program. In 1728 and 1729, hostile Indians attacked recently established San Ignacio mission, but the attacks ended following a punitive expedition. In 1762, raids by Indians against San Francisco de Borja, established in the same year, also resulted in another punitive expedition. The resistance to the mission reportedly originated with shamans (*hechizeros/curanderos*), and the role of shamans in opposition to the mission program appears in many documents written by the missionaries.

The expansion of the mission frontier in the 1770s, 1780s, and 1790s to the northwestern Pacific coastal plain called La Frontera was also met with resistance on the part of the Indians. Dominican missionary Luis Sales, O.P., the author of an important account of the expansion of the Dominican mission frontier, reported resistance. According to Sales, the exploration for potential mission sites "was happily accomplished with many sudden assaults on the part of the heathen[.]" The Indians wounded Sales and a number of soldiers in the attacks. In March of 1804, hostile Indians killed two soldiers in the mountains near San Vicente mission.

In order to establish the new colonial order in the peninsula, the missionaries, working in conjunction with the soldiers, had to eliminate the influence of traditional leaders, particularly shamans, and win the hearts, minds, and bodies of the Indian converts. Two missionary accounts record examples of how the missionaries undermined the authority of traditional leaders and attempted to win the loyalty of Indian converts. Following the 1762 punitive expedition against hostile Indians north of San Francisco de Borja, missionary Wenceslao Linck staged a mock punishment. The corporal who commanded the punitive expedition condemned the Indian prisoners to a punishment of twenty-five lashes over consecutive days, which were to be administered publicly as an example to recent Indian converts. At a prearranged moment at the beginning of the punishment, missionary Linck intervened to request suspension of the punishment, but only after several had already been whipped. The same strategy was used for the next seven or eight days, thus breaking down the will of the prisoners to resist further.

Dominican missionary Sales described in specific terms the methods he used to undermine native support for shamans. On one occasion Sales had a shaman beaten with iron rods in front of other Indians. At another time Sales ordered a soldier to "make a pretense of thrusting a sword into his [a shaman's] breast, and on seeing the gesture the old man started to cry out and to run. Later we caught him and gave him a few blows, asking him beforehand if he would feel pain. He answered 'no' and was given two or three wacks, whereupon he began to yell and scream like a madman. The operation over he ran away, joined his people, and told them that he had not wanted to draw upon his power, that if he had wished he could with his saliva have put us all to death, and the Indians believe it because he tells them so."

The Indians brought under varying degrees of control in the missions continued to resist the changes in lifestyle being enforced by the missionaries. In the first years following the establishment of missions, the missionaries often blamed shamans for stirring up trouble among the converts. This is best documented through a discussion of resistance in the missions established in the southernmost Cape district.

Between 1720 and 1737, the Jesuits established six missions among the Indian groups of the southern part of the peninsula, including the Cape district. Indians in the Cape district mounted the most serious opposition to the Jesuit mission program. In 1723, 1725, and 1729, troops were sent from Loreto to suppress what the missionaries reported to be restlessness among recent converts. This reported discontent was only a portent for more serious resistance a few years later.

In 1734, a large-scale uprising broke out in the Cape district, requiring two years and the deployment of troops from Sinaloa to suppress it. The well-coordinated uprising reportedly led by shamans resulted in the destruction of four missions and the death of two Jesuit missionaries and a number of soldiers. Moreover, twelve sailors from a Manila galleon were killed in an ambush when the ship stopped at San Bernabé, the port of San José del Cabo, for resupply. An estimated 3,000 Indians died as a direct consequence of the uprising, but the military intervention from Sinaloa had other long-term consequences for the Indian population. The soldiers reportedly spread syphilis among the Indian population through sexual liaisons with Indian women, and the unchecked spread of the malady contributed to the rapid demographic collapse of the Indian population.

A second rebellion broke out in 1740 among a group known as Perícues living in the Cape district near San José del Cabo. The Indians launched an attack near the presidio established at San José del Cabo following the previous uprising. Following the attack, most of the converts living at San José fled from the mission into the nearby mountains. A military expedition from Loreto presidio suppressed the uprising after some fatalities, and officials exiled seven Indian leaders to central Mexico. This was the last serious rebellion in the Cape.

The suppression of the first wave of resistance to the mission regime proved fairly effective in Baja California. In contrast to the Pimería Alta and other frontier mission districts in Spanish America, secondary resistance in the form of large-scale uprisings was limited in the peninsula. There were, however, instances of unrest at individual missions, often in response to excessive social control by individual missionaries. In 1784, for example, there was unrest at Santa Gertrudis and San Francisco de Borja because of excessive punishment at the hands of the Dominican missionaries stationed at the two missions.

The most serious instances of secondary resistance occurred in the northwestern Dominican missions in the 1830s, as the mission system began to collapse in the peninsula. In 1831, Indians living at Santa Catalina mission rebelled and waged a guerrilla campaign against the military for about a year. In 1837, fugitive Indians from San Miguel mission reportedly organized a raid by Quechans from the Colorado River against the missions. In 1840, rebellions occurred at Santa Catalina and Guadalupe missions.

Manuel Rojo interviewed Jatinil, an influential Indian chief who led the uprising at Guadalupe mission. This recorded oral history account provides a rare native perspective on the causes for resistance in the peninsula missions. Jatinil could best be described as an ally of the missionaries, and his band had helped to build Guadalupe mission in 1834. Attacks by hostile Indians apparently forced Jatinil's band to migrate to the coast and establish a fortified village at El Descanso. Jatinil revolted because of forced conversions of members of his band by Dominican Félix Caballero, one of the last missionaries stationed in the missions. Jatinil and his warriors chased Caballero out of Guadalupe, and the Dominican subsequently fled south.

There were other forms of resistance in the missions, including the murder or attempted murder of missionaries, flight, and the destruction of mission property. Converts living in the Baja California missions murdered several missionaries, and attempts were made on the lives of others. In the 1730s, a shaman shot an arrow at Jesuit Franz Wagner, missing the missionary by inches. The shaman was executed and his body hung in public as an example to others, and other Indians involved in the assassination attempt were whipped. In 1803, Indians killed two missionaries and a soldier at Santo Tomás in the span of five months. Four Indians involved in the murders were eventually apprehended.

Flight was perhaps the most common form of Indian resistance in the Baja California missions. One of the best documented cases of large-scale flight is from two of the Cape missions: Todos Santos and San José del Cabo. In 1768, Visitador General José de Galvez ordered the relocation of more than 700 Guaycurans from San Luis Gonzaga and Dolores del Sur missions located in the Magdalena Desert to Todos Santos. Galvez ordered the relocation of the indigenous population of Todos Santos to San José del Cabo. The purpose of his plan was to increase the population of Indian converts at missions with greater agricultural potential, and to close missions located at sites with marginal potential. In relocating the Guaycurans, however, Galvez expected a radical change in lifestyle. In the Magdalena Desert missions the Guaycurans still largely supported themselves through the collection of traditional foods, supplemented by grain produced at the two missions or imported from Sinaloa and Sonora. At Todos Santos, the Guaycurans were expected to become a disciplined labor force.

In the five years following the relocation of the Guaycurans to Todos Santos a severe measles epidemic killed more than 300 people, and many of the survivors fled from the mission. In 1771, 170 Indians remained on the mission rolls and of those, 30 reportedly were fugitives. In 1773, 49 still were fugitives and 3 had been banished to San Francisco de Borja mission, and in the following year 11 were still absent from the mission. Discontent took other forms. In 1770, a delegation of Guaycurans went to Loreto to complain about the corporal punishment being used by a hired overseer to discipline Guaycurans workers. Moreover, they complained that the Franciscans stationed at the mission would not allow them to collect wild foods.

Francisco Palou, O.F.M., the chronicler of the Franciscan years in Baja California, noted other forms of Guaycuran resistance at Todos Santos. He wrote that "but few remained, because of the great number of deaths in the epidemics that had occurred at that mission; that the few who had remained had not settled down but constantly ran away; and that in the mission they do nothing but destroy property, stealing everything they can not sparing even sacred things, for they had just stolen a silver cruet from the church." The forms of passive resistance that Palou attributed to "ungrateful" behavior were related to the traumatic changes that occurred following relocation to Todos Santos. A handful of Indians from San José del Cabo also were reported absent in 1774.

Flight was also a problem in the Dominican missions established in the northwestern part of the peninsula after 1774. Sales described in graphic terms the problem of Indian flight and the measures taken to stop it: "If they [converts] run away from the church and the troops, they are hunted down, taken from their forests and beaten. And though they are caught a hundred times and well beaten, still they run away, and they are always found at the same spots."

A variety of sources provide evidence of flight. Entries in the burial registers for the missions record the deaths away from the missions of baptized Indians, as well as of unbaptized Indians during epidemics. Between 1777 and 1805, there were burials of 93 Indians away from

Rosario mission. The largest group entry was on December 1, 1782, and recorded the deaths of 35 converts who had fled from the mission during an epidemic. Rojo recorded that, following the murder of two missionaries at Santo Tomás in 1803, a large group of Indians fled to the Colorado River delta to the east of the mission. A group of soldiers sent to return the fugitives had to retreat when they became trapped in swampy terrain.

Manuel Rojo recorded the account of Janitin, an Indian convert who recalled his capture and settlement at one of the northern missions. Shortly after being baptized, Janitin was put to work in the fields at agricultural tasks that were new to him. The missionary had Janitin flogged when he did not perform his work assignments as expected, and in response Janitin tried to escape. Janitin then described his recapture by soldiers:

> I found a way to escape; but they followed my trail and caught me in La Zorra; there they [soldiers] lassoed me like the first time and took me to the mission, martyrizing me on the way; when we arrived the father was walking the corridor of the house, and he ordered them to tie me to the pillory and punish me; they gave me so many lashes that I lost consciousness.... I was several days without being able to get up from the ground where they laid me out, and I still have the marks from the lashes that they gave me at that time on my back.

The Baja California mission program was based upon a new regime of social control designed to eliminate practices contrary to the religious, social-cultural, political, and economic objectives of the missionaries and the colonial state. Only a handful of sources allude to different measures of social control implemented by the missionaries.

As already discussed, the missionaries took extraordinary measures to undermine the influence of shamans. This also included the elimination of traditional religious practices, including dancing associated with cycles in the annual harvest, such as the maturation of fruit, which also had social importance. The missionaries associated them with pagan religious practices, but also viewed dances as being potentially subversive to the stability of the mission regime. Sales recorded steps taken in the northern missions to stop dances:

> [I]f perchance the missionary hears of it and sets out for the dance with his soldiers to break it up they all flee. One seizes the drum, another as much seed as he can carry, and they go into hiding in the brush. Such action by

action by the missionary is very useful (but not always safe since they take certain chances, as happened to me in the beginning when with a sling-shot they dislocated a bone) for preventing the killings and other disorders and also to prevent worse results of the dance since, as they are brought together from many places, they are wont to plot to fire the mission and to rob or kill the missionary. If the soldiers went alone without the missionary to interfere with the function there would be very bad results.

Flight was a problem in the missions, and evidence indicates that missionaries maintained dormitories to incarcerate converts at night. Dormitories were also a common feature of the later mission regime in Alta California. In the 1740s Jesuit Antonio Tempis reported that he separated young children from their parents for indoctrination, and housed them in a dormitory close to the residence of the missionary. Manuel Rojo wrote a detailed description of the use of dormitories in the northern peninsula establishments that emphasized the segregation of the Indian population according to civil state, and the incarceration at night of single women in dormitories: "When the prayers were finished they would shut them up inwards according to the social state of each; the married ones slept apart with their wives in a ward destined for all of them, the single men in another ward, and the single women in the unmarried women's quarters, the key to which was kept by the missionary in his cell."

The missionaries managed the population of Indian converts through incentives and punishments, particularly corporal punishment. Several missionary accounts make reference to the use of corporal punishment. The Jesuit Johann Baegert described forms of punishment in his account written following the expulsion of the Jesuits in 1768:

> Their talent for feigning a sudden and severe illness and letting themselves be carried over many miles to the mission could almost be called a custom. A good whipping, however, would quickly restore most of them to health. . . . The reason for such make-believe and disgusting lies is either to escape work, which they hate so much, though it is sometimes for their own good, or to escape punishment which they may incur for their villainous actions. . . . For all other misdeeds the culprit is either given a number of lashes with a leather whip on his bare skin, or his feet are put into irons for some days, weeks, or months.

The Franciscan chronicler Palou wrestled with the issue of corporal punishment in his discussion of Guaycuran resistance. The Spaniards continued to use a pseudoethnic term to identify this group of neophytes, because they had not made the transition to indio status. In 1770, a delegation of Guaycurans went to Loreto to complain about the excessive punishments employed by the overseer hired on José de Galvez's orders to administer the mission. Palou claimed that the Indians had made up the story, but then stated that the Guaycurans had been punished on the orders of the missionary. Finally, Palou charged that one of the Guaycurans had beaten himself in order to blame the overseer. Sales, in discussing discipline in the northern missions, wrote that the Indians were gathered daily at the missionaries' house, where "faults were reprehended, and they are beaten with whips."

The use of corporal punishment to discipline converts living in the missions forms a central theme in the account of Janitin, mentioned above. According to Janitin, only recently brought to the mission: "In the afternoon they whipped me because I didn't finish the job they gave me, and on the following day the same thing happened to me as happened the day before; every day they whipped me unjustly because I didn't do what I didn't know how to do[.]"

Indian Resistance in the Pimería Alta Missions

An analysis of Indian resistance in the Pimería Alta concerns two distinct patterns that at times merged: resistance by northern Pimas congregated into the missions, and raids by groups such as the Apaches and Seris that were on the margins of Spanish settlement. Rebel Pimas at times joined up with Apaches and/or Seris to raid missions and ranches. Spanish officials developed different policies to cope with escalating levels of raiding, which inhibited the settlement of northern Sonora, and categories to define hostile indigenous groups.

Northern Pimas converts staged two revolts against the colonial system being set up in Sonora. The first revolt, in 1695, was an example of primary resistance, a response to changes initiated with the introduction of the Jesuit mission system. In particular, the employment of Opata overseers in the newly established missions caused friction, since the Opatas viewed the Pimas in a condescending fashion. The brutal treatment by the frontier military of Pimas accused of stock raiding exacerbated tensions.

The 1695 uprising began at Tubutama mission, and initially involved one Pima faction defined by Spaniards by a distinct pseudoethnic term,

"Piato." The rebels killed the Opata overseer and his assistants at Tubutama, and moved on to Caborca where they killed the Jesuit missionary. Initially, the uprising was limited in scope, and missionary Eusebio Kino, S.J., arranged a meeting at a place called El Tupo with the rebels and other Pima leaders to end the uprising. However, the meeting degenerated into a massacre by Spanish soldiers of Pimas present including individuals who had not been involved in the initial uprising, and the rebellion escalated. A large force of Pimas destroyed the missions at Tubutama, Caborca, Imuris, and San Ignacio. A large Spanish force was sent into the Pimería Alta, but the rebel Pimas had already dispersed. Kino negotiated a second agreement that restored peace, but it took several years to restore the devastated missions and start the Jesuit program again.

The second major uprising occurred in 1751, and was an example of secondary resistance organized and led by a hispanicized Indian leader named Luis Oacpicaquigua from Saric. Oacpicaquigua had participated as an auxiliary in a 1750 punitive expedition against the Seris in southern Sonora, and in recognition of his services was named captain general of the Pimas by the governor of Sonora, an artificial honor. The poor performance of the Spaniards in the expedition against the Seris apparently convinced Oacpicaquigua that the Pimas could expel the settlers and missionaries from Pimas territory, and he organized an uprising that drew greatest support from the Pimas in the older western Pimería Alta missions. The uprising began with the massacre of 18 settlers at Saric, and by the time that Spanish forces had captured Luis, 2 missionaries and about 100 settlers had died.

Suppression of the revolt in 1751 did not end northern Pima resistance. In 1756, rebel Pimas reportedly joined Seris in the Cerro Prieto range in southern Sonora and participated in raids on missions and Spanish settlements. Rebel Pimas also joined Apache bands in raids against the Pimería Alta as well. In the mid- and late 1750s, the rebels targeted the western Pimería Alta missions, where the 1751 rebellion had been centered. In 1756, for example, sixteen rebel Pimas and one soldier died during an attack against Pitiqui *visita* (satellite village) of Caborca mission. Raids against Oquitoa left seven dead.

The two Pima uprisings did not represent a united front against Spanish colonization, but rather resistance by certain factions. The patterns discussed above, however, do reflect responses to Spanish colonization. The 1751 revolt in particular was a clear rejection of the colonial order being created by the Spaniards. Following his capture, Oacpicaqigua leveled a series of charges against the Jesuits that were discounted after a cursory investigation by the governor of Sonora. Pima discontent in the 1750s was probably also related to growing Spanish settlement in the region.

Raids by Seri and Apaches posed a serious challenge to the Spanish in Sonora as well, and threatened the stability of the colonial order being created on the frontier. The Seri, nomadic hunters and fishermen, occupied an inhospitable territory along the coast of the Gulf of California in southern Sonora, as well as Tiburón Island. The Spanish initially attempted to attract Seri to missions, and in 1679 the Jesuits established a mission in southern Sonora for the Seris named Santa María del Pópulo. Over the next sixty years a number of Seris lived at Pópulo although they represented only a small percentage of the Seri population.

Beginning in the 1720s, Seri not living on the mission at Pópulo raided Spanish ranches in southern Sonora. There were also conflicts with pearl fishermen in the Gulf of California, and contacts with pearl fisherman may have been responsible for the growing hostility of the Seris. In 1740, Seri became involved in the Yaqui revolt.

Spanish action led to the disruption of the mission program at Pópulo and an escalation of warfare with the Seri. In 1748, the government ordered the relocation of a military garrison to Pópulo, and disputes over land and water rights between the garrison and Seri at the mission led to protests by leaders of the Seri at the mission. Spanish officials responded to the Seri protests by arresting eighty families and deporting the arrested women to Guatemala and elsewhere in New Spain. The Seri at Pópulo revolted and fled to the Cerro Prieto range.

Seri joined with rebel Pimas and Apaches to raid the Pimería Alta, but Seri bands also raided throughout Sonora. Spanish officials viewed the Seri as a serious threat, and organized several large military expeditions that initially did not give the desired results. In 1750, a force of 520 Pima auxiliaries and frontier troops invaded Tiburón Island and the Gulf coast Seri territory, but the expedition did not end Seri raiding. In 1768, a force of 1,100 soldiers chased Seri and rebel Pimas in the Cerro Prieto range, and on Tiburón Island. There was another expedition in 1769. After 1769, Seri and rebel Pimas began to surrender, and continued military pressure in the 1770s forced the remaining Seri to stop fighting. By 1780, most had settled in several missions.

Raids on the Spanish frontier from Sonora to Texas by indigenous bands collectively known as the Apaches posed a far more serious threat to the stability of the colonial regime being created in northern Sonora. Until the late 1760s, the target of most Apache raids was herds of livestock, especially horses. With the exception of two bloody attacks in 1757 and 1770, few people actually died in Apache raids. A 1757 attack on San Lorenzo, close to San Ignacio mission, resulted in thirty-two deaths. Similarly, a 1770 raid on Sonoita visita of Guevavi mission resulted in nineteen deaths. Most raids were similar to two 1758 attacks on Cocospera and Soamca missions that netted the Apaches 80 and 100 horses respectively.

With the exception of the two raids described above, most victims of the Apaches in the Pimería Alta were individuals or small groups caught on the roads in the region. Moreover, fatalities at the hands of the Apaches accounted for only a small percentage of deaths. Between 1755 and 1760, a total of 62 people reportedly died in the Pimería Alta at the hands of hostile Indians: 49 settlers, most in the attack on San Lorenzo, 9 Pimas, and 4 Yaquis and *nijoras* (Indian slaves). From 1743 to 1766, Jesuit missionaries recorded 439 burials at Guevavi, one of the most exposed mission communities, but only 5 of the dead were killed by Apaches. Similarly, between 1768 and 1825, the Franciscans stationed at Guevavi and Tumacacori recorded 653 burials, but only 41 were victims of hostile Indians, including the 19 killed in 1770 during the raid on Sonoita visita.

What impact, then, did Apaches raiding on the Pimería Alta have during the first six decades of the eighteenth century? A series of mission inventories from the 1730s through the 1760s provide one possible answer. The inventories reported numbers of mission livestock, generally the more or less tame animals kept in corrals or on the open range close to the missions. Inventories also reported large numbers of uncounted livestock, especially cattle, on the open range. The evidence suggests that Apaches targeted the tame animals at the missions and ranches, especially horses, which entailed less effort than rounding up livestock from the open range. Since the Jesuits and settlers already sold livestock in the local mining camps and elsewhere, the theft of tame animals was a significant economic loss.

The inventories also recorded the number of livestock at each of the missions, and the documents show that, despite raids, the missions still had numbers of livestock, and some growth in the size of their herds. The first example is San Francisco del Bac mission. In 1737, the mission reportedly owned 240 cattle, 200 sheep and goats, 394 horses, and

2 mules. Twenty-eight years later, in 1765, the number of cattle had grown to 334, sheep and goats increased to 536, the horse herd had been reduced to 152 animals, most likely due to Apache raids, and the mission owned 19 mules. Similarly, Guevavi mission experienced a growth in the number of livestock, with the exception of horses. From 1737 to 1761, cattle increased from 240 to 870, sheep and goats from 200 to 1,270, but horses and mules dropped respectively from 108 to 95 and 40 to 27.

Warfare with the Apache bands in northern Sonora and surrounding jurisdictions escalated from the late 1760s through the early 1790s. The relocation of the Sobaipuri Pimas from the San Pedro Valley to the Santa Cruz Valley missions facilitated Apache raids into the Pimería Alta. In the following decades there were a number of spectacular Apache raids on Pimería Alta settlements. On November 19, 1768, a large raiding party attacked Soamca mission. The raiders burned most of the buildings and defiled the church. Nobody died, but the raiders wounded four Pima converts. A second attack on Soamca on April 11, 1769, left the remaining buildings in ruins. In November of 1779, a band of about 350 Apache warriors passed close to Tucson presidio and was attacked by soldiers from the garrison. Three years later, on May 1, 1782, another large Apache band attacked Tucson presidio. Three Spanish soldiers were wounded, and at least eight of the attackers died.

The Spanish policy toward hostile Indians also shifted beginning in the late 1760s and the 1770s. There was more coordination between presidio commanders and frontier governors in campaigns against Apaches, and more punitive expeditions were launched, putting considerable pressure on the different Apache bands across the frontier. In 1776, the royal government created a new military and administrative jurisdiction in northern New Spain called the Provincias Internas, and experimented with relocating presidios. Finally, in the late 1780s, Viceroy Bernardo de Galvez initiated a new policy that gave the Apaches only a choice between war or peace, with no possibility of temporary truces that in the past had allowed them to regroup. The government also offered scalp bounties.

The increased military pressure forced Apache bands to surrender in the early 1790s and agree to settle in a type of reservation system near several presidios. As a part of the new policy the Spanish attempted to increase Apache dependence on trade goods, liquor, and inferior firearms, as well as rations provided to those bands settled at the presidios.

In 1793, 107 Apaches settled at Tucson presidio, and the government allocated 1,600 pesos per year to provide rations of corn, meat, tobacco, and sweets. The Apaches settled at Tucson were allowed to keep their firearms, and local officials reportedly looked the other way at minor stock raiding.

The Apache peace lasted in the Pimería Alta until about 1831, when political turmoil in central Mexico and the fiscal insolvency of the newly created Mexican government undermined the reservation system that had been weakened during the Mexican independence wars (1810–1821). Some Apaches rioted after 1810 in response to the reduction of rations, and others resumed stock raiding. Nevertheless, the Spanish in the Pimería Alta also scored notable successes in relations with Apaches between 1810 and 1820. In May of 1819, a band of 236 Apaches surrendered at Tucson, and two months later, in July, ten more bands surrendered. With the resumption of warfare in the 1830s and the inability of Mexican military officials to cope with Apache raids, the population and economic growth in northern Sonora that had begun in the 1790s was undermined. Settlers suffered heavy casualties in the raids and abandoned a number of communities. Even the presidios were not immune. Between 1832 and 1849, Apaches reportedly killed 200 people at Fronteras.

Resistance and Raiding in Texas

Indigenous responses to Spanish colonization in Texas were similar to those described above for northern Sonora: raids by groups from the southern plains such as the Apaches and Comanches; rebellion; flight; and the refusal to go along with the Spanish agenda. Throughout most of the eighteenth century the Spanish military in Texas battled raids by Comanches and Apaches, and settlements and particularly the missions were built for defense as typified by the five San Antonio area missions. Walls surrounded the missions, and bastions were built at the corners of the defensive walls. The Indians living on the missions, mostly Coahuiltecans caught between Apaches and Comanches, sought refuge in and helped defend the missions from hostile attacks.

At different periods during the eighteenth-century, Spanish policy toward the Apaches and Comanches shifted. In 1749, officials in San Antonio negotiated a peace with Lipan Apache bands and for the next two decades attempted to induce Apaches to settle on missions. However, the Apaches made peace with the Spanish in order to get help in their ongoing conflict with the Comanches, their bitter enemies. The Apache-Comanche hostilities led to the destruction of the first mission established for the Apaches. In 1758, a large force of Comanches and allied tribes destroyed San Saba mission, established in the previous year. In the early 1760s, the Franciscans established two more missions for the Apaches, but the outcome was similar to the San Saba debacle. In both instances the Apaches refused to settle on the missions, and once again the Comanches began raiding the two missions when they discovered their location. These raids forced the Franciscans to abandon the missions, and in the 1770s the Spaniards resumed hostilities against the Apaches.

A new chapter in Spanish-Indian relations opened in 1785, when Spanish officials from San Antonio negotiated a peace treaty with Comanche band leaders. The Spanish had now abandoned the idea of trying to convince Great Plains Indians to settle on the missions and had introduced a new policy based on trade and subsidy. For the next several decades the Spanish and Comanches cooperated in attacks on the Lipan Apaches, and Spanish officials attempted to increase the economic dependence of the Comanches on Spanish trade goods and defective firearms.

Indians living on the missions in Texas rebelled against the authority of the missionaries in both active and passive forms. The situation of the Coahuiltecans in the San Antonio missions was unique, because, as noted previously, they were caught in the chronic warfare between Apaches and Comanches and heavily depended on the Spanish for defense. However, other groups did resist the mission regime. The Karankawa bands on the Gulf Coast offer the best examples. For nearly a century (1720s–1820s) Franciscan missionaries attempted to convince the Karankawas to settle on the missions and abandon their traditional way of life, which included seasonal transhumance between permanent village sites on the coast and inland. Eventually the Franciscans established three missions for the Karankawas: Espíritu Santo (1722, moved several times); Rosario (1754); and Refugio (1793). The Franciscans stationed on the San Antonio missions also recruited converts from the coastal bands.

The Karankawas' resistance to the mission program took several forms. Flight was the most common, but the Karankawas did not permanently abandon the missions. Rather, they fit them into the established pattern of seasonal transhumance and used the missions as an additional source of food in years when traditional foods may have been scarce. Karankawas came to and left the missions, frequently on a seasonal basis, and the missionaries complained bitterly that the military would not return the fugitives. Censuses for the three missions document short-term seasonal shifts in the number of Indians actually residing on the missions. The surviving baptismal register for Refugio mission shows examples of children born to Indian parents previously baptized at one of the missions, being baptized months and even years after their birth. The parents, who had left the mission, allowed the children to be baptized only once they returned to the mission, and the baptism of the children was in effect the price for being allowed to come to the mission after having been absent for a time.

Karankawa resistance was also violent. There are many reports of attacks on the missions by Karankawa bands and the theft of mission livestock. The Spanish soldiers, not familiar with the topography of the Gulf Coast, did not dare to pursue the raiders. There was also one major rebellion at one of the missions established for the Karankawas. In 1779, a baptized Indian led an uprising that forced the abandonment of Rosario mission for a decade. The rebel leader eventually returned to the mission and helped rebuild the community.

The other pattern of indigenous responses to the Spaniards can be characterized as indifference to the mission program. This best describes the way in which the Hasinais of east Texas approached the evangelization efforts of the Franciscan missionaries. The Franciscans operated missions among the Hasinais between 1690 and 1693, and again from 1716 to the early 1770s with a short hiatus following a French attack from Louisiana in 1719. In the earlier period the Franciscans attempted to force village chiefs to abandon polygamy, and shamans blamed the presence of the Franciscans for an epidemic and drought. The Franciscans abandoned the Hasinais missions under considerable duress.

The second round of the mission program among the Hasinais proved to be equally frustrating for the Spaniards. The Hasinais and other neighboring peoples traded with the French, and obtained the firearms that the Spaniards would not provide. Conversion proceeded slowly, and most baptisms were of people who were dying. The figures on total baptisms at three missions as recorded in a 1768 report highlights the failure of the Franciscans to convert the Hasinais. The Franciscans at Adais mission reported 103 baptisms of Indians, and 256 baptisms and 116 burials at the nearby presidio. The total was 11 baptisms as against 7 burials at Ais mission, and 12 baptisms and 8 burials at Guadalupe mission. Not surprisingly, the Spanish government ordered the closing of the east Texas missions in the early 1770s following the French transfer of Louisiana to Spain after the Seven Years' War (1755–1763). The strategic need to hold east Texas against the French no longer existed, and the expense of maintaining Franciscan missionaries and a military garrison could not be justified in light of the failure to convert the Hasinais.

There was an added complication to the story of Hasinai-Spanish relations. One of the survivors of the 1758 attack on San Saba reported hearing some of the Indians speaking Tejas, the Spanish term for the language spoken by the Hasinais. Hasinai warriors from east Texas may thus have taken part in the destruction of San Saba as allies of the Comanches.

Indian Resistance in Alta California

The Spanish occupation of Alta California also met with considerable resistance from the very beginning. The rape of Indian women by soldiers provoked attacks, but so too did the Spaniards' practice of letting their livestock graze on fields of food-producing plants maintained by the Indians. San Diego, established in 1769 and the first Spanish settlement in the region, was the focus of considerable Indian resistance, and the Franciscans built the first mission complex for defense. In 1769, Kumeyaay warriors attacked the settlement, and resistance culminated in a large-scale 1775 raid by warriors from a number of villages that resulted in the destruction of the mission and the death of one missionary and a handful of Spaniards.

Franciscan reports from other missions describe similar resistance. In 1771, for example, Kumi.vit leaders attacked San Gabriel mission twice. The Spaniards uncovered another plot to attack the mission in 1779, and thwarted an attack in 1785 lead by a female Kumi.vit shaman named Toypurina. The resulting trial record provides important insights into the motives for Indian resistance. Toypurina told her captors that she wanted to expel the Spaniards from her land.

A new pattern of resistance emerged among converts either born at the missions or who had lived on the missions for a number of years. A number of resistance leaders had served as *alcaldes* (Indian civil officials) on the missions. Perhaps the best known was Estanislao from San José mission, who headed a village of runaways located in the San Joaquín Valley in the late 1820s until attacked by

Mexican soldiers. Eventually Estanislao returned to San José mission. Another was Cipriano from Santa Clara mission, who led a separate band of apostate Indians.

The most serious uprising occurred in 1824 at Santa Bárbara, La Purísima, and Santa Inés missions located in Chumash territory. The excessive flogging of an Indian at La Purísima was the immediate catalyst for the revolt, but the probings of Chumash religious beliefs by Franciscan missionary Señan threatened the secret world of the ?antap cult. Hundreds of Indians resisted for more than a month, and some 400 fled into the San Joaquín Valley and established a syncretic society that blended traditional Indian and Spanish cultural elements. The community survived until the late 1830s, until wiped out by a severe epidemic.

In addition to the uprisings, flight was a common form of resistance. The record is replete with reports of flight by small and large groups of Indians that numbered into the hundreds. Some fugitives avoided recapture by military expeditions sent after them, and by the 1830s as many as 1,900 Indians had successfully escaped from the missions. Letters reporting flight can measure the importance of Indian labor to the Franciscans. In 1798, 138 Indians fled Santa Cruz mission. The Franciscan reporting the flight to local military officials complained of a shortage of labor at the mission.

Because of the unique economic relationship between the California missions and the government, which stipulated production of surplus food for the military, the Franciscans imposed strict social control. They used corporal punishment to enforce discipline. The puritanical missionaries also believed that, unless controlled, the Indians would engage in sexual liaisons. As a consequence, the Franciscans directed the construction of dormitories to segregate unmarried men and women. Descriptions of the dormitories include references to unhealthy conditions, including poor sanitation, which damaged the health of the men and women locked up in them at night. The detailed record of building construction from annual reports shows that the missionaries had dormitories built for women almost from the beginning of each mission, and that they added dormitories for single men at a later date when flight became a serious problem. The unhealthy conditions in the dormitories contributed to high mortality rates among women, rates considerably higher than for men. This, in turn, helps to explain the demise of the Indian populations living on the missions.

Conclusions

The missionaries stationed on the missions throughout northern New Spain envisioned a radical change in indigenous culture, social relations, worldview and religion, and economy and gender labor roles. The native peoples in all of the regions discussed here resisted in a variety of active and passive forms. In some instances the Indians scored short-term victories, as was the case in the 1680 New Mexico Pueblo uprising. Indian raids by such groups as Comanches and Apaches effectively stopped Spanish expansion, but the Indians already on the missions never successfully forced the abandonment of entire mission frontiers. The Spanish frontier military managed, just barely, to maintain a degree of control over the Indian populations, and scored notable victories against raiders from beyond the frontier. The resistance, however, did not end until the demise of the mission system, and mission residents managed to preserve to a certain extent traditional values in the new missionary "utopia."

Chapter 5

The Demise of the Indian Populations in the Missions

The decline or demographic collapse of the native populations of Mexico's northern frontier was one of the most important consequences of Spanish colonization, and was directly related to the organization of mission communities. This chapter examines the causes and manifestations of depopulation, as well as definitions of race and status, and how the Spanish fit the indigenous population into their definition of society. Topics considered include contact population size, the dynamic of congregation and the formation of the mission communities, the causes of population decline, and case studies of demographic patterns on the missions. The chapter concludes with a discussion of race and status, and the place of the indigenous population in the Spanish vision for a colonial society.

Contact Population Size

In recent years scholars have debated the size of native populations in 1492, or shortly before the first sustained contact with old world populations. The sources for estimating contact populations include firsthand European accounts of the societies they encountered, and inferences drawn from the number and size of settlements documented in a given region either archaeologically and/or in written sources. The range of estimates can be considerable, and at best the "numbers" game is an imprecise exercise in arriving at educated guesses of what might have been. A number of perceptions can color the scale of estimates. For example, scholars who emphasize the sophisticated level of Indian civilization and the destructive consequences of European conquest tend to make higher estimates. On the other hand, proponents of a sanitized "white legend" view that minimizes the consequences of the European intrusion into the Americas tend to make smaller population estimates, leading to the conclusion that Indian population decline, and therefore the effects of European colonization was not significant. At best, estimates are educated guesses, and their utility lies in suggesting ranges of possibilities rather than precise totals.

A second difficulty in estimating contact population sizes is defining the unit of the estimate. Is an estimate for a village, a collection of villages, a tribe, a band, or a region bounded by natural features such as river and mountains? Moreover, there is an added complication in assessing the demographic consequences of Spanish colonial policy. Indians brought into the emerging Spanish colonial society passed through the mission communities. Records left by the missionaries are the most complete and accurate. However, in many instances not all residents of a village or members of a tribe or band relocated to the missions. Some scholars have used mission records as the basis for estimating contact population size, and these estimates rely on the use of arbitrary conversion ratios of the number of Indians baptized to the total population in a given area.

One final factor to consider in discussing estimates of contact population size is the level of social-political organization of the native societies. Early contact accounts, which contain other forms of bias, frequently describe village, tribe, or band size. But the Indian societies being described ranged from the sedentary and stratified Pueblos of New Mexico to the Coahuiltecan hunter-gatherers of northeastern Mexico and Texas. Other groups on the northern frontier of Mexico practiced varying forms of agriculture or plant food management supplemented by hunting and gathering activities, and occupied different and generally permanent village sites on a seasonal basis. The northern Pimas of Sonora and Arizona, for example, practiced agriculture, but also left their primary settlements in a pattern of seasonal migration to exploit wild plant foods or for communal hunting expeditions. The Karankawas of the Texas Gulf Coast migrated on a seasonal basis between permanent village sites on the coast and slightly in the interior. Contact accounts used to describe Indian societies and especially the size of native populations could easily miss large numbers of people temporarily or seasonally absent from principal settlements.

THE DEMISE OF THE INDIAN POPULATIONS 91

The following are the most recent or generally accepted estimates for the size of the native populations of northern frontier New Spain. The population of the New Mexico Pueblos may have been as high as 80,000 around 1598, prior to the establishment of the first permanent Spanish settlement. Scholars generally recognize that fifty years of intermittent Spanish contact with the Pueblos beginning with Francisco de Coronado's 1540–1542 invasion led to population losses through warfare and the introduction of disease, and resulted in the abandonment of some communities. Disease may have also spread north from central Mexico prior to 1598 along established trade routes, although scholars disagree on the extent of contacts between central and northern Mexico and the frequency of epidemics reaching as far north as New Mexico during the sixteenth century.

Estimates for the contact populations of Texas and southern Arizona pose several problems. Only a small percentage of the Indians living in both areas came under Spanish control, and hence into the historical record. At the height of the Texas mission system in the 1760s, some 1,500 converts lived in the mission communities. However, the total number of Indians congregated onto all of the missions established in Texas during the period of Spanish occupation was considerably higher. The example of the three missions established for the Karankawas and neighboring groups along the Gulf Coast (Espíritu Santo—1722, Rosario—1754, Refugio—1793) demonstrates the hazard of making population estimates. The Karankawas probably numbered several thousand when the Spaniards first arrived in Texas. The Franciscan missionaries assigned to Texas attempted to permanently settle Karankawa bands on the missions, but largely failed to modify an established pattern of seasonal migration. Karankawas came and left the missions seasonally, and the mission censuses represented only the number of Indians who happened to be at the mission when the census was prepared. The appended population graph of Rosario and Refugio missions shows considerable shifts in population in the 1790s, when the missionaries prepared a number of censuses. The changes occurred seasonally. Estimates for the population of Sonora ranges as high as 85,000 in 1530, and some 5,000 to 10,000 in southern Arizona south of the Gila River.

Baja California, a largely arid peninsula, supported a relatively sparse population. Estimates range from 40,000 to 60,000 when the Jesuits established the first missions. Scholars, particularly the late Sherburne F. Cook, closely examined all possible evidence to arrive at estimates for the size of the California Indian populations in 1769, when the Franciscans under the direction of Junipero Serra, O.F.M., established the first mission. Cook's estimate of some 300,000 for the area within the modern state of California has been accepted by several generations of scholars as being reasonable. Again, as in the case of Texas, the Spanish missionaries only congregated a small percentage of the total native population of California on the missions. Moreover, patterns of resettlement were complex. The Franciscans first relocated the Indians living in the coastal valleys where they established the missions, and then congregated Indians from different groups living in the interior valleys. The population of the groups living in the coastal zone may have been as high as 60,000. Between 1769 and 1832, the Franciscans baptized some 88,000 Indians in all of California. This suggests that the missionaries resettled 20,000 to 30,000 Indians on the missions from interior groups.

The Process of Congregation

Scholars have attempted to explain why the different native groups living on the frontier of northern New Spain agreed to live on the missions, and particularly why they left their traditional way of life to move to the mission communities. A number of explanations have been suggested, including the novelty of the new material goods brought by the Spaniards, the native perception of the missionaries as being powerful intermediaries to the spirit world, and the usefulness of the Spaniards as allies. In Baja California, the missionaries took control of the best sources of water, and used bluff and intimidation. The Coahuiltecans of Texas had little option but to go to the missions, caught as they were between the escalating war of the Comanches and Apaches. The missionaries also used techniques to persuade the Indians to accept baptism. They quite aggressively challenged and undermined the authority of traditional native leaders, particularly shamans. They also took children to use as leverage over parents. The anthropologist Daniel Reff recently argued that in Sonora, following the devastating epidemics of the sixteenth century that disrupted native society and killed many traditional leaders, the Jesuit missionaries provided a convenient point of reference for social and political reorganization. The Jesuits and later the Franciscans took advantage of a pattern of seasonal migration practiced by the Pimas between the river valleys where the missions operated and water holes in the hinterland. Bands of Indians called "Papagos" by the

THE DEMISE OF THE INDIAN POPULATIONS 93

missionaries came to the missions seasonally to work in the harvest and to share the crops of the villagers living in the river valleys; the missionaries pressured the migrants to remain.

The California missions provide perhaps the most complex explanation for the motives for resettlement on the missions. Initially, Indians, particularly lower-status individuals, may have been attracted by the new material goods offered by the Spaniards, the novelty of something new, and the possibility of gaining higher status in the new society being created. As more and more Indians entered the missions, traditional networks of trade, intervillage marriage, and political-economic alliances collapsed. Within the missions, the presence of soldiers was an intimidating factor. The landscape outside of the missions was no longer as friendly since many people already lived in the missions. The Franciscans also used techniques similar to those employed in other parts of the frontier. They targeted the families of village leaders for conversion, and often took children to use as leverage over parents, or wives to use as leverage over husbands. As Indians ran away, the soldiers sent to recapture them "punished" the non-Christians who may have helped the fugitives. Once enticed to the missions by the presence of family members, individuals were pressured by missionaries to accept baptism.

A recent debate has examined drought as a factor motivating Indians to settle on the missions. The debate has focused on the Chumash, who entered five missions located in south-central coastal California. The argument focuses on drought destroying traditional plant foods, and El Niño climatic changes wiping out important fisheries. It is known that shortages of traditional food sources forced Chumash onto the missions. However, an analysis of mission crop records shows that drought was not severe enough to destroy water-sensitive plants for prolonged periods of time. Variations in ocean water temperatures may have disrupted fisheries to the point of forcing mass migration to the missions by the Chumash villagers who had previously relied on fish as their primary source of food. Yet the record of drought, based on the analysis of tree rings, does not provide compelling evidence for a cause-and-effect relationship between shortages of traditional plant foods and resettlement on the missions. Wheat and corn production fluctuated. Ultimately, a variety of factors contributed to the variation in crop size from year to year, and the mission reports contain few references to severe drought.

A more compelling argument can be made that the growing numbers of cattle and sheep destroyed the carefully cultivated plots of seed-producing plants relied upon by the Indians, and ate ripe acorns that formed the staple for most California Indians. During the early years of colonization disputes arose when Spaniards pastured their livestock on lush fields of what to them appeared to be wild plants, fields carefully managed by the Indians. Moreover, as the herds grew, the missionaries distributed the cattle and sheep to different locations within the mission territory. Mission reports record the rapid growth of the herds that found abundant pasture, and few natural enemies. Growing numbers of cattle and sheep ranging across Chumash territory probably hastened resettlement on the missions. The two graphs recording the number of cattle and sheep on the missions among the Chumash show large increases in the size of the herds between 1800 and 1810, which was also the period of the last great hiatus to the missions.

Most of the missions established in Texas proved to be failures, because the Franciscan missionaries could not convince or force the different native groups to abandon their traditional way of life. The Hasinais of east Texas, for example, already practiced agriculture, and had access to European trade items including firearms from the French in Louisiana. The Spanish offered the Hasinais few benefits, and alienated the chiefs by insisting they abandon the practice of polygamy. Similarly, the Lipan Apaches refused to modify their hunting economy to become sedentary farmers. Status in Lipan society came with success as a hunter and warrior, and the cultivation of crops was very similar to the collection of wild plant foods, which was a task for women. Work in the fields would seriously erode the status of the hunter and warrior. The Lipan Apaches established a semblance of peaceful relations with the Spaniards and promised to settle on missions, but apparently were only interested in embroiling the Spaniards in conflict with their traditional enemies the Comanches. Only Coahuiltecan band members readily accepted resettlement on the five San Antonio missions, seeking refuge there from raids by both the Apaches and Comanches. Moreover, the missions probably offered a more secure food supply that could be easily obtained without having to hunt and gather in small groups over wide areas, a practice that left the Coahuiltecans particularly vulnerable to mobile Apache and Comanche war parties.

As discussed previously, the Franciscan effort to congregate the Karankawas on the missions lasted for about a century, and ultimately failed because the missionaries could not change the Karankawas' tradi-

THE DEMISE OF THE INDIAN POPULATIONS 95

tional way of life. The Franciscans generally blamed the failure of the Karankawas mission program on the lack of support from military and civil officials in Texas and the fickle nature of the Karankawas themselves. The frustration of the missionaries over their failure to congregate the Karankawas was reflected in several reports on conditions in Texas in the middle and late eighteenth century. Writing in the 1780s on conditions at Espíritu Santo mission, Friar José López, O.F.M., noted that

> [n]early as many natives have fled to the coast and woods, both from among those who were brought there, and from those who, born in the mission, were induced by the bad example of the coastal Indians to follow them. Neither the clamor nor the supplications of the missionaries have been successful in obtaining repressive measures from the Governor of the Province to put a stop to the almost daily escapes (even when these occur in his presence).

A more detailed examination of the congregation of the Karankawas and Lipan Apaches highlight the origins of these frustrations. The Karankawas were hunter-gatherers who occupied seasonal camps on the coast and along streams and rivers in the coastal prairie environment. The availability of different food resources defined seasonal migration within a clearly defined territory. During the fall and winter Karanakwa bands occupied large camps on the coast to exploit estuarine foods, particularly redfish and black drum. During the spring and summer, Karankawas occupied smaller camps on the coastal prairie and hunted bison, deer, and other animals, and collected plant foods. Large deposits of artifacts and food remains, particularly at the coastal sites, indicate long-term occupation of camps. Seasonal migration figured into decisions by bands to enter the missions established for the Karankawas. The Franciscans located both Rosario and Refugio missions in the coastal prairie environment at locations that best suited plans for the development of agriculture and ranching. Most documented instances of Karankawa bands moving to the two missions occurred during the spring, which coincided with the traditional occupation of camps in the coastal prairie.

The Franciscan missionaries never broke the pattern of seasonal migration between the coast and coastal prairie, and they frequently complained about how the Karankawas left the missions to return to the coast, and in fact abandoned Rosario en masse in 1779, forcing the abandonment of the mission for a decade. This was a problem at Rosario mission, which was located well outside of the traditional territory of the Karankawas on the lower San Antonio River (near present-day Goliad). Karankawas leaders told the Franciscans that they would be more willing to settle at Refugio mission, which was located within their territory. One important factor in the continued independence of the Karankawas was the inability of Spanish troops to follow runaways from the missions in an estuarine environment they were not familiar with. Moreover, the soldiers did not have boats to follow the Karankawas to offshore islands.

Censuses show considerable short-term fluctuation in the populations of both Rosario and Refugio missions. Moreover, a number of the fluctuations can be directly tied to the traditional pattern of seasonal migration. For example, in June of 1779, 254 Indians reportedly lived at Rosario (see figure 5.1). This coincided with the period when the Karankawas returned to the coastal prairie. In December of 1798, however, the number was down to 70, which was the period when the Karankawas returned to the coast. The gender and age structure of the mission populations provides additional evidence of the patterns of migration from the missions. A 1794 census of Rosario mission recorded a total of 18 men, 25 women, 29 boys, and 20 girls. Other censuses from both Rosario and Refugio show more boys than girls, roughly equal numbers of men and women, but only a small number of unmarried men at Rosario in the 1790s. The Rosario and Refugio censuses show a trend of gender imbalance among children, and the absence of men from the mission, particularly unmarried men, who apparently left with greater frequency.

A surviving set of baptismal and burial records from Refugio mission for the years 1808–1828 provide additional evidence. There was an under-registration of burials, which suggests that many Karankawas baptized at Refugio later died away from the mission. The majority of the baptisms were of young children, including some children born to adults previously baptized and brought to the missions months or in one case several years after birth. Moreover, the majority of baptisms of converts were of children: few adults converted and received baptism.

The evidence shows that the Karankawas did not adopt a sedentary life in the missions. Rather, they incorporated the missions into the seasonal migration between coast and coastal prairie as an additional potential food resource and most likely came to the missions when

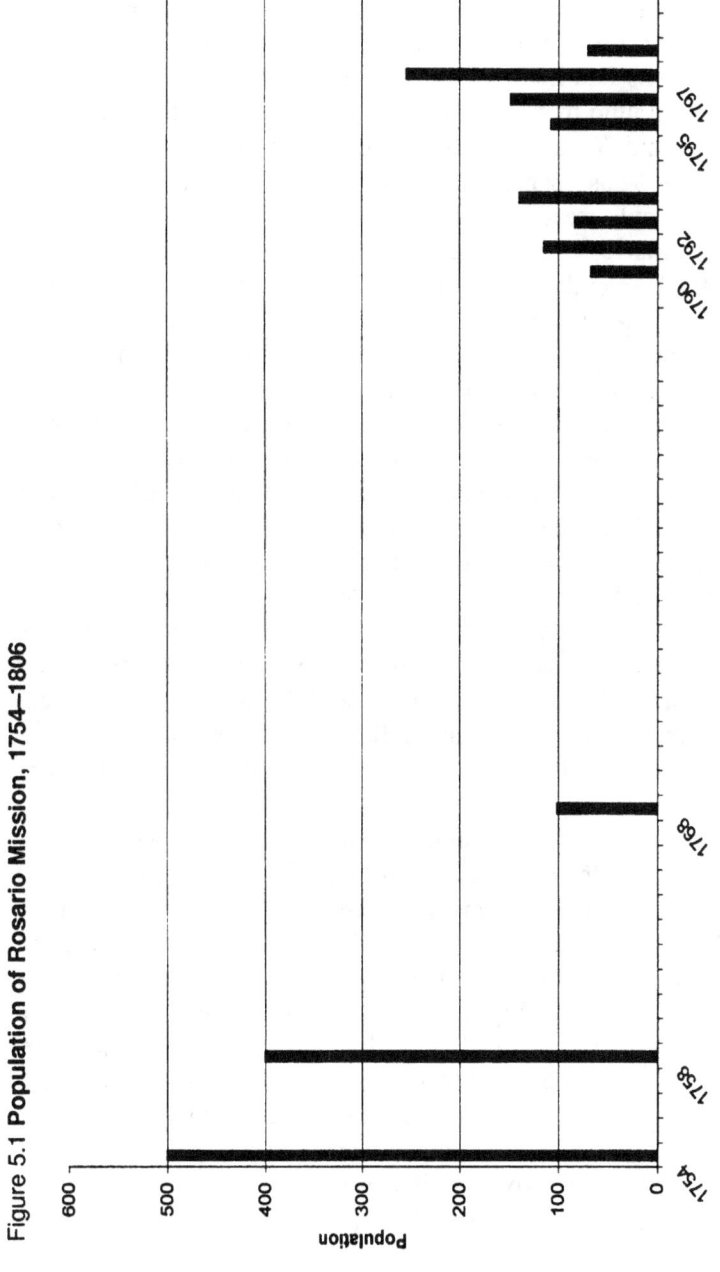

Figure 5.1 **Population of Rosario Mission, 1754–1806**

Source: Data compiled from Robert H. Jackson, ed. *New Views of Borderlands History*. Albuquerque: University of New Mexico Press, 1998, p. 153.

traditional sources of food were scarce. Moreover, the proliferation of herds of cattle and other livestock probably displaced wild game such as deer and bison. The decline in game made the choice for the natives to come to or remain outside of the missions permanently or periodically somewhat more difficult. By the 1770s and 1780s, Espíritu Santo and Rosario missions had herds of 15,000 and 30,000 cattle respectively, and in 1808 Refugio mission counted 5,000 cattle and small livestock. On the other hand, Karankawas could kill and eat mission livestock, and as early as the 1750s Spanish military officials expressed concerns that Karankawas would steal mission animals.

The missionaries encountered similar difficulties with the Lipan Apaches. After several decades of war, Spanish officials in Texas made peace with the Lipan Apaches, who were already being attacked by Comanches moving into the southern plains. In 1758, Comanches and allied tribes destroyed San Saba mission, established for the Lipans in the previous year, but Spanish officials maintained a large garrison at San Saba after the destruction of the mission. Lipan band chiefs continued to request the establishment of missions, and one chief known as Gran Cabezón promised to settle 300 members of his band at a new mission. The commander of San Saba presidio assigned troops to protect new missions for the Lipans that were to be established on the Nueces River, and Franciscans from the Apostolic College of Santa Cruz de Querétaro staffed the new establishments named San Lorenzo and Candelaría founded on January 23, 1762, and February 6, 1762, respectively. The presidio commander and college officials established the two new missions without the formal authorization of the viceregal government, and without government funds.

Initially, about 400 Lipans settled at the two missions, but they also came and went as they pleased to go hunt bison or because of food shortages at the missions. Raids on Lipan *rancherias* (villages) in the Nueces River area by Comanches and allied tribes in 1762 forced the Lipans to leave the missions, but some Indians did return. In 1764, a smallpox epidemic killed Lipans at the missions. In October of 1766, a force of 300 Comanches directly raided the missions for the first time, and periodically returned to attack the missions. By the summer of 1767, the Lipans abandoned the two missions and never returned.

In 1766, the Marqués de Rubí, conducting an inspection of frontier presidios, visited the two Apache missions. Rubí reported the presence of thirty soldiers from the San Saba presidio at San Lorenzo, a site he deemed poorly defended. The soldiers defended four missionaries, but there were no Apaches. In Rubí's judgment the missions were a waste of resources. Archaeological excavations of the San Lorenzo mission site, located on the top of a small ridge close to the Nueces River, have shown that the mission structures, built of adobe, surrounded a rough square enclosed by walls that included two bulwarks. However, from the perspective of a military expert, the defensibility of the San Lorenzo mission complex must have been limited.

Keeping Indian converts, especially hunter-gatherers, in the mission communities was a problem in other parts of Texas as well as other sections of the frontier. The process of radically transforming the way of life of native peoples led to disaffection, and flight was a particularly attractive form of resistance. The Franciscans stationed on the five San Antonio missions reported instances of individual and group flight, and a set of guidelines written in the late 1780s for missionaries stationed on La Purísima Concepción mission discussed the need to periodically visit the Gulf Coast to track down fugitives. Flight was also a significant problem in the California missions.

The Indian populations living on the mission communities generally were unable to grow through natural reproduction, and gradual population decline would have resulted had it not been for the congregation of new converts. Thus missionaries in Sonora, Texas, and the Californias aggressively sought new recruits and at times employed frontier troops to help round up the new recruits.

The relationship between population size and the process of congregation can be seen through two case studies from Texas and California. The first is San Antonio de Valero (the Alamo) established in 1718. The Franciscans stationed at San Antonio mission witnessed a decline in the numbers of new recruits after the 1750s. From 1727 to 1746, baptisms of new converts totaled 273, and in 1746 the population of the mission reached around 390. Over the next thirty-four years the number of new converts dropped to only 131, and the population experienced a net decline of about 290. Similar patterns occurred at San Antonio mission in California established in 1771. The Franciscans actively congregated Indians from the Salinan population living in the Salinas Valley and neighboring Santa Lucía mountains, until about 1810. During this period the Franciscans baptized 2,026 converts and 1,354 children born at the mission, and recorded 2,270 burials. The recorded maximum population of 1,296 was in 1805, and in 1810 the numbers stood at 1,122.

Over the next eighteen years (1811–1828) the Franciscans baptized 763 newborn children and recorded 1,191 burials. The population dropped to 710 in 1828. Over the next six years the Franciscans baptized a small number of Central Valley Yokuts, but the decline in the mission population continued. In 1834, when the government secularized the mission, only 567 Indians remained (see figures 5.2 and 5.3).

Detailed demographic studies of the New Mexico missions based on parish registers have yet to be completed, but the available evidence suggests a very distinct pattern. The Pueblos exercised a greater degree of autonomy from the control of the missionaries, particularly in the eighteenth century. Moreover, Pueblo leaders probably exercised more control over such decisions as the incorporation of outsiders into the communities. Finally, the available evidence does not suggest that the Franciscan missionaries carried out large-scale congregation programs as in Sonora, Texas, and the Californias. The population of the Pueblos declined, but then stabilized and grew. In 1679, the population was about 17,000; it was 10,568 in 1750, reached a nadir of 9,732 in 1800, was 9,923 in 1820, and grew to 16,510 in 1842 (see figure 5.4).

Causes of Population Decline

Conventional analysis identifies epidemics of old world diseases as the leading cause of the decline of the Indian populations living in the missions. Disease certainly was an important factor, but on closer examination other factors emerge. Studies of historical European populations in many instances document a pattern of increased births following a major mortality crisis. The so-called rebound rarely occurred in the mission communities of Texas, northern Sonora, and the Californias. Rather, epidemics exacerbated a problem of chronically high infant and child mortality rates as reflected in low mean life expectancy rates (MLE) for children born on the missions.

Different factors contributed to unhealthy conditions in the mission communities. Settlement in the missions entailed significant changes in lifestyle, social organization, and gender roles, among other things. These changes were particularly traumatic for hunter-gatherers, who experienced the greatest changes in every aspect of their lives. For example, the drive to establish economic self-sufficiency in the missions required sustained labor by Indian converts, and in some instances the mission labor regime required men to perform work they perceived to

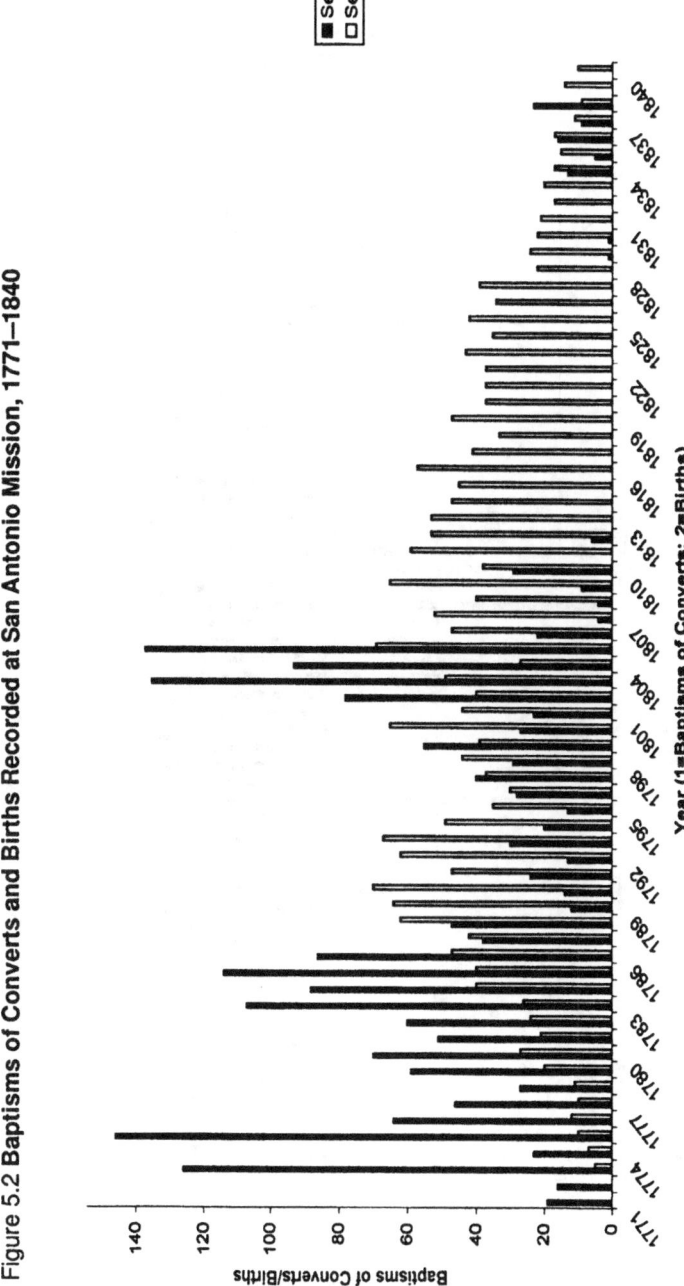

Figure 5.2 Baptisms of Converts and Births Recorded at San Antonio Mission, 1771–1840

Source: Monterey Diocese Chancery Archive, Monterey, California.

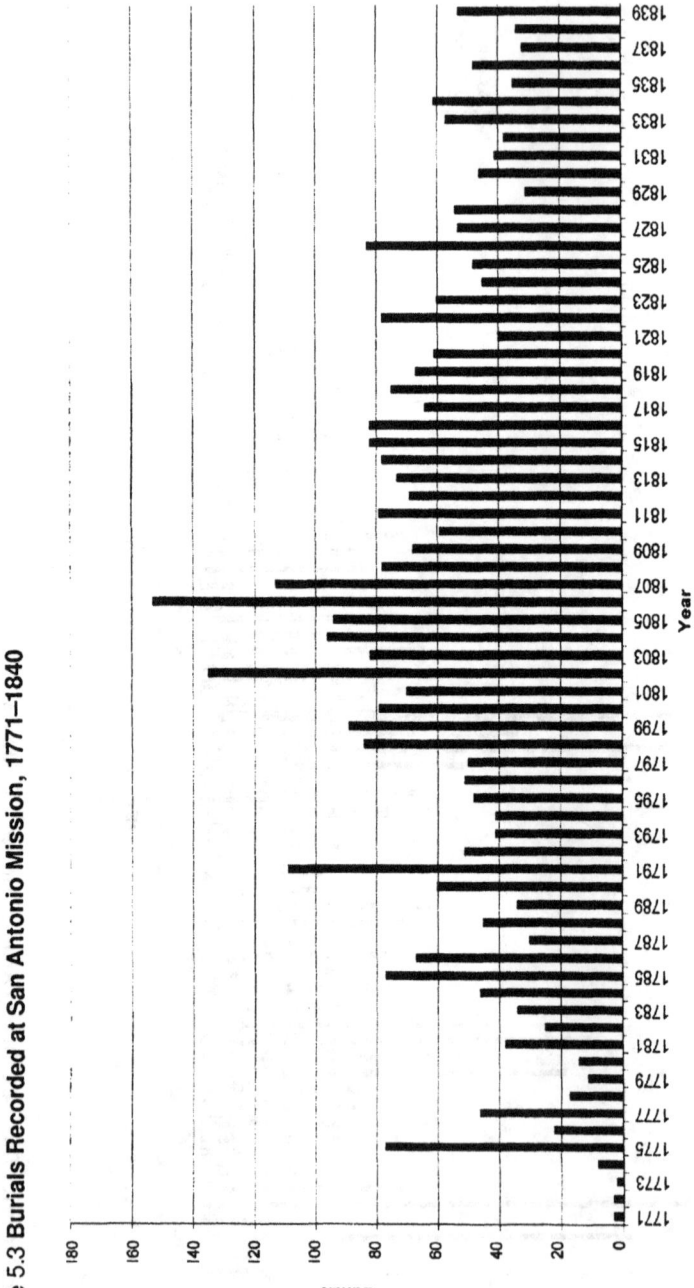

Figure 5.3 Burials Recorded at San Antonio Mission, 1771–1840

Source: Monterey Diocese Chancery Archive, Monterey, California.

Figure 5.4 Indigenous Population of New Mexico, 1598–1821

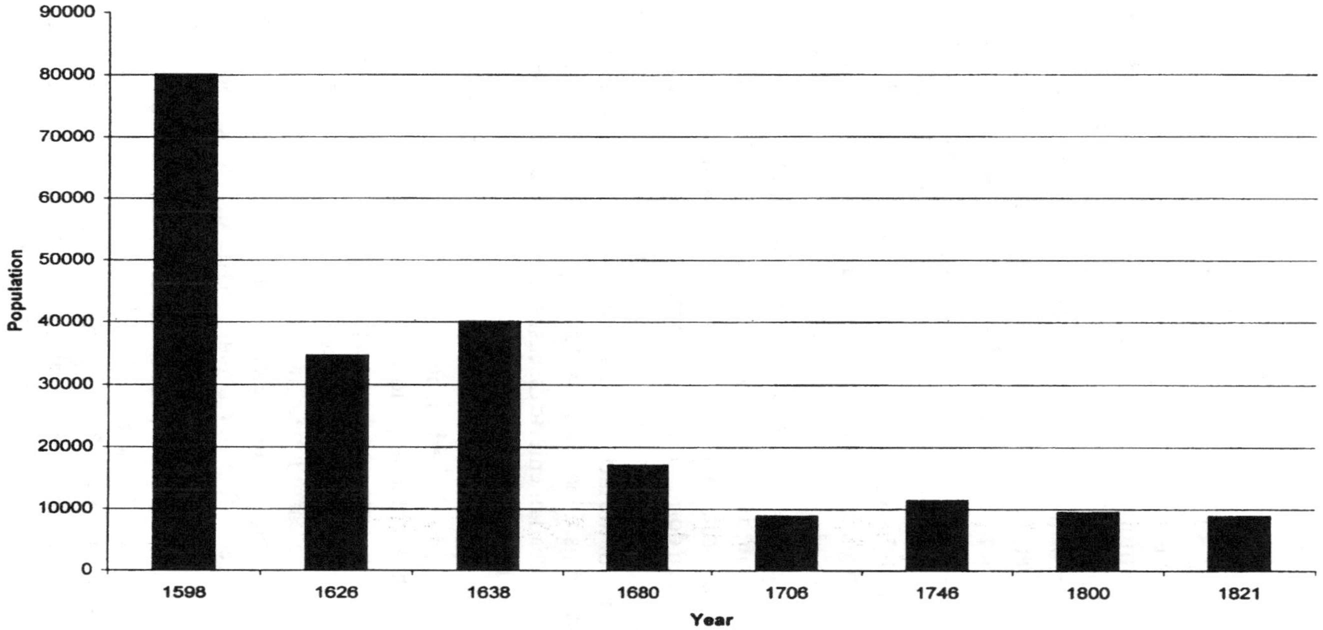

Source: Data compiled from Robert H. Jackson, ed. *New Views of Borderlands History.* Albuquerque: University of New Mexico Press, 1998, p. 67.

be best suited for women. In many instances, particularly in the California missions where the Franciscans made significant contributions to support the local military, the missionaries used corporal punishment to maintain labor discipline. Public punishments were not only physically painful but also humiliating, and could undermine the status of the convert subjected to disciplinary action.

In the California missions the Franciscans suspected sterile Indian women of practicing abortion and infanticide, and devised an extremely humiliating form of punishment that has been recorded in rather graphic terms in several oral history accounts given by former residents of the missions. Women believed to have aborted pregnancies were given a *novena* (lashes for nine consecutive days). Moreover, they were made to wear leg irons and stand in front of the church before and after mass holding an ugly wooden doll representing the aborted child. Such extreme practices in the missions helped to traumatize many Indians.

Physical living conditions in the missions also contributed to health problems. Higher population densities facilitated the spread of disease. Indian housing is frequently described as being crowded and unsanitary. In California, and perhaps in other mission groupings, where missionaries used dormitories to segregate and control segments of the Indian population, such as unmarried women and girls, descriptions of the dormitories tell of the lack of toilets and the stench of human wastes, among other problems. Finally, the water supply was easily polluted, contributing to the spread of enteric diseases, and venereal disease spread among the natives living at the missions.

The missionaries, who in most instances had little or no formal medical training, had limited means of combating disease. Moreover, in the seventeenth, eighteenth, and early nineteenth centuries, medicine was still based on ancient Greek principles and the humoral and miasma theories. Information from fifteenth-century medical texts was still distributed in the early nineteenth century. The germ theory did not gain general acceptance until the end of the nineteenth century. Finally, the cures used were often worse than or as deadly as the disease. Toward the end of the eighteenth century the Spanish government introduced inoculation by variolation—the infection of an individual with pus from a smallpox pustule in the hope that the inoculated individual would contract a mild infection. This method did significantly reduce mortality rates during smallpox epidemics. On the other hand, records from the California missions mention the importation of mercury pills for the

THE DEMISE OF THE INDIAN POPULATIONS 105

treatment of syphilis, and missionaries used it to treat various sexually transmitted diseases common among Indians. While mercury may have brought the symptoms of syphilis under control, it is also a deadly poison.

Degree of Population Decline

As already discussed, contact population estimates are not reliable enough to accurately document the precise rate of decline of the Indian populations on the frontier colonized by the Spaniards. However, a notion of the dynamic of Indian depopulation can be gained from an examination of demographic trends in the missions. I briefly examine here population movements in the Pimería Alta missions of northern Sonora, the five establishments in San Antonio, Texas, along with the Karankawas missions and the establishments in the Californias. This is followed by a discussion of Pecos, one of the mission pueblos in New Mexico.

The Jesuits opened the Pimería Alta mission frontier beginning in the late 1680s, and then the Franciscans who later replaced them continued to congregate numbers of new converts well into the first decades of the nineteenth century. The missionaries drew upon the population of northern Pimas known as Papagos, who occupied the desert west of the river valleys where the missions operated. Moreover, as the population declined during the course of the eighteenth century, the missionaries depopulated villages and relocated the surviving converts to the central mission communities known as *cabeceras*. In 1761, 4,088 Indians lived in 22 villages under the jurisdiction of the missionaries, but the numbers dropped to 1,312 living in fourteen villages in 1806 and 1,127 in the same number of villages in 1820. A detailed analysis of one village, Tumacacori, provides additional insights into the process of depopulation. In most years death rates were higher than birthrates, and mean life expectancy at birth was below 20 years in most years. The population of the village fluctuated with the ebb and flow of congregation of new converts, but stagnated and declined as birthrates lagged behind death rates (see figure 5.5).

The Indian populations of the five San Antonio, Texas, establishments grew through the 1750s, as the Franciscans continued to congregate new converts. Once the number of converts dropped off, the mission populations also declined. In 1756–1758, the population of the five missions totaled 1,321. The numbers dropped over the next 60 years. In 1777, there were 757 Indians living in the five missions, 353 in 1790, and in

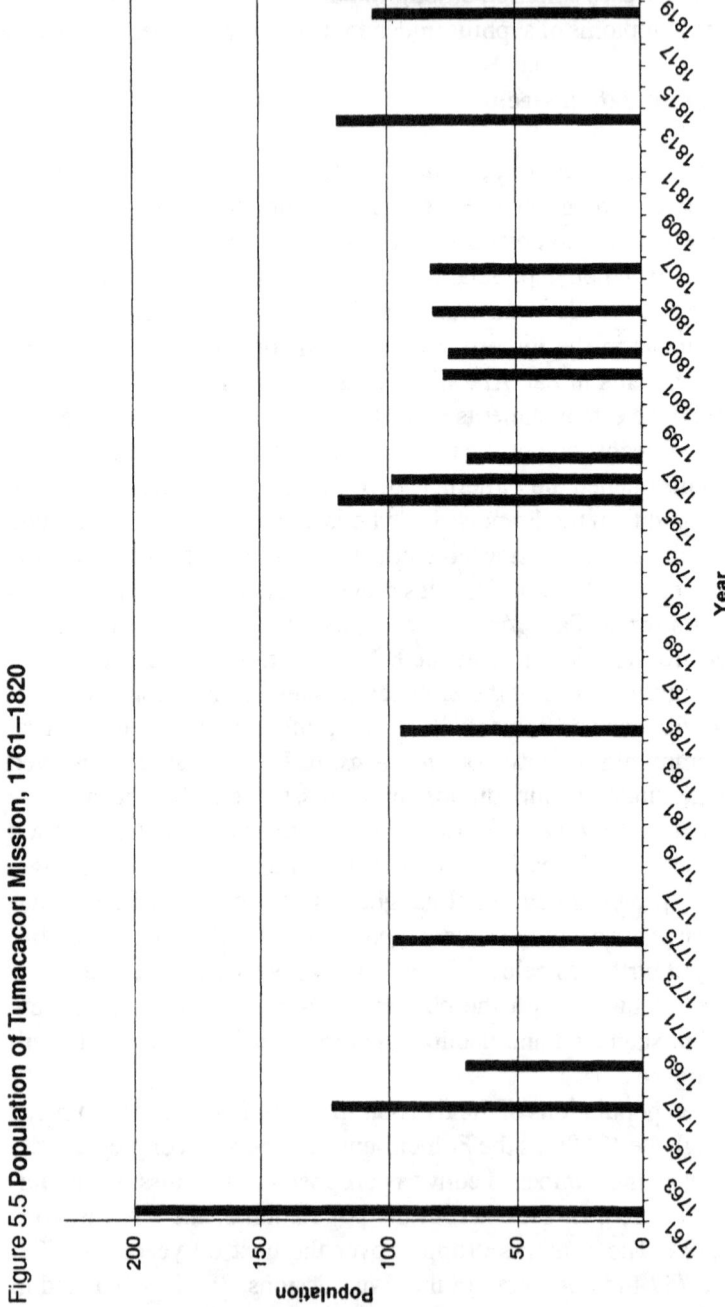

Figure 5.5 **Population of Tumacacori Mission, 1761–1820**

Source: Data compiled from Robert H. Jackson, *Indian Population Decline: The Missions of Northwestern New Spain, 1687–1840.* Albuquerque: University of New Mexico Press, 1994, 168.

1815 a mere 107 in the four surviving establishments. The government had already closed San Antonio de Valero in 1794. The vital statistics of the population congregated there tell the story. Death rates exceeded birthrates, averaging 75 deaths per thousand (1727–1781) as against 32 births per thousand.

As already discussed, the population of the three missions established for the Karankawas on the Texas Gulf Coast experienced considerable instability due to the persistence of the well-established pattern of seasonal migration, and instances of rebellion and other forms of resistance such as flight. The population of Espíritu Santo, established in 1722, fluctuated between about 400 and 100 from the 1740s to the 1790s. There were some 400 Indians living on the mission in 1747, 178 in 1758, 300 a decade later in 1768, 103 in 1787, and 50 in 1822. Similarly, the populations of Rosario and Refugio also fluctuated. In the first mission the population numbered some 500 in 1754, 101 in 1768, 254 in June of 1797 before the summer migration to the coast, and 62 in 1805. The number of converts at Refugio went from a low of 43 in February of 1795 during a period of difficulties with Karankawas bands to a high of 224 in December of 1804, after the fall migration to the interior.

The Jesuit, Franciscan, and Dominican missionaries stationed on the Baja California missions congregated most of the Indians on the missions, but the mission communities were inviable. The population of the missions grew as long as there were potential converts living outside of the missions, but they declined once the congregation program tapered off. In 1755, 5,974 Indians reportedly lived on thirteen missions, and in 1768, 7,149 lived on fifteen, but the numbers dropped to 3,156 on eighteen missions in 1800 and 2,815 on the same number of establishments in 1804. Some of the older Jesuit missions experienced short periods of growth through natural reproduction in the 1750s and 1760s, largely because the Jesuits were successful in limiting contacts between the peninsula and mainland of Mexico. However, the expulsion of the Jesuits in 1767–1768 coupled with the organization in the peninsula of the 1769 expedition to Alta California combined to break the relative geographic isolation of the missions. Personnel moved across the length of the peninsula, and epidemics spread more rapidly and with greater effect than during the Jesuit period. The mission populations rapidly declined after 1768, as reflected in the vital rates of San José de Comondu mission established in 1708. Prior to the 1760s Comondu was a high fertility and high mortality population, and mean life expectancy ranged between ten and twenty years. Birth and death rates were high, but after an initial period of decline the numbers increased through natural reproduction. After the Jesuit expulsion birth rates dropped, death rates remained high, and mean life expectancy at birth dropped to below ten years. By the first decade of the nineteenth century the population of Comondu fluctuated between only twenty and thirty people, and in the mid-1790s children under age nine made up only 5 to 9 percent of the total population. Within several generations the indigenous population would disappear as birthrates dropped and few children survived to replace the adults that died.

The next case is Alta California (see figure 5.6). Until the 1820s, the Franciscans increased the populations of the missions by establishing new communities and congregating large numbers of new converts from tribelets located at increasing distances from the mission communities. In 1790, 7,711 Indians lived on 11 missions, 18,680 on 19 missions in 1810, and 21,063 on 20 missions in 1820. Over the last fifteen years of the mission system, however, the number of converts entering the missions dropped, and mission populations declined. In 1825, 20,301 lived on 21 missions, and nine years later in 1834 there were 15,225 in the same number of settlements. Mortality rates were chronically high on the California missions, and birthrates low. Santa Cruz mission, established in 1791, presents the worst case scenario for mortality and Indian depopulation on one of the California missions. Death rates were high: the crude death rate was often 100 per thousand population, and averaged 89 per thousand. In contrast, crude birthrates averaged only 26 per thousand, and the average rate of decline was 67 per thousand population per year. Mean life expectancy at birth, another gauge of the health of a population, fluctuated between slightly more than one year to between four and five years at birth. A comparison can be made with the population of the four presidios established in California. Birthrates were consistently higher than death rates, and the population grew. Mean life expectancy at birth ranged between twenty and forty years, much higher than for the Indian populations living on the missions.

The population of the New Mexico Pueblos declined between the sixteenth and the early nineteenth centuries. At the time of the 1680 Pueblo revolt, there may have been 17,000 Pueblos. Following the reoccupation of New Mexico in the 1690s, the population fluctuated: there were some 8,840 in 1706; 9,432 in 1800; and 8,852 in 1821. Not

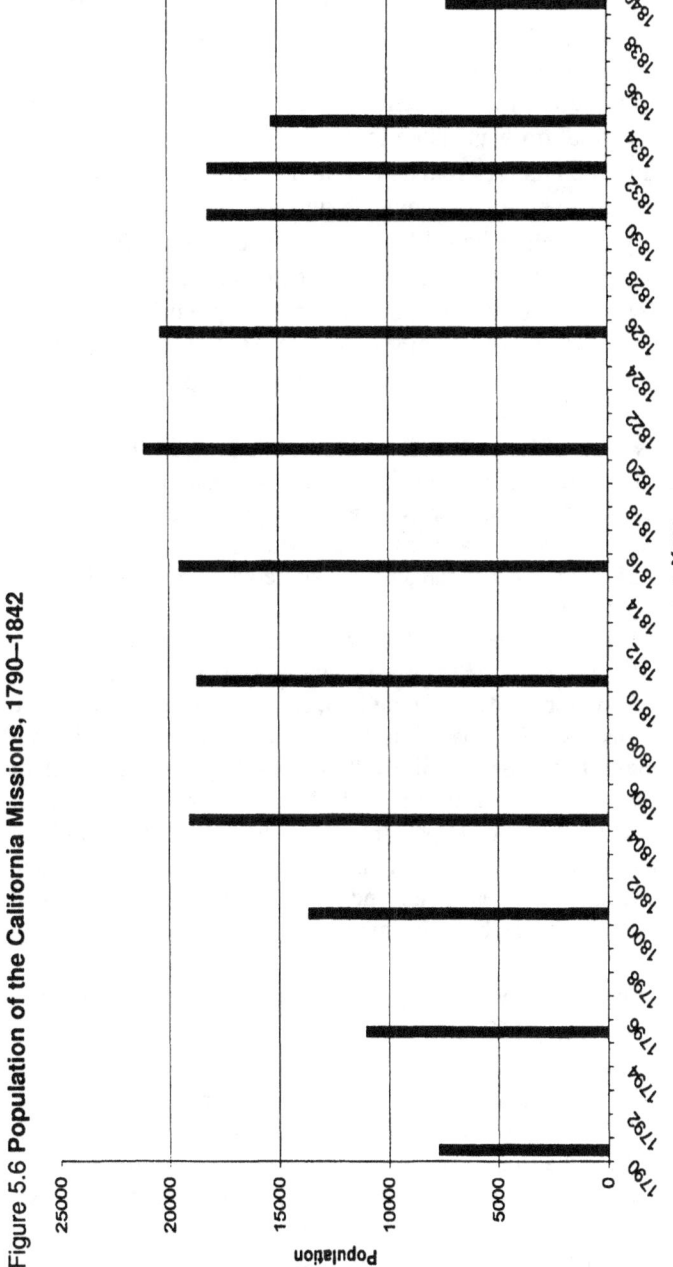

Figure 5.6 **Population of the California Missions, 1790–1842**

Source: Data compiled from Robert H. Jackson, *Indian Population Decline: The Missions of Northwestern New Spain, 1687–1840.* Albuquerque: University of New Mexico Press, 1994, 60.

only did the population of the Pueblos decline, so too did the number of actual settlements. More than eighty Pueblos were abandoned following the arrival of the Spaniards. The cause for the decline in the number of settlements is complex. In part it was related to Spanish policy. In 1609, officials in Mexico City directed the missionaries to congregate the indigenous population into a smaller number of villages. Decline of the indigenous population was also a factor, as were drought and raids by hostile Indians such as the Apaches. Apache raids were largely provoked by the Spanish settlers of New Mexico themselves, who raided Apache villages for slaves to be sold in the mining camps in Chihuahua.

The so-called Salinas province missions located east of Albuquerque and east of the Manzanillo mountains offer an example of the complex factors contributing to Pueblo abandonment. A 1669 report described problems faced by the Pueblo communities in Salinas province:

> One of these calamities is that the whole land is at war with the widespread heathen nation of the Apache Indians, who kill all the Christian Indians they find and encounter. No road is safe; everyone travels at risk of his life, for the heathen traverse them all, being courageous and brave, and they hurl themselves at danger like people who know no God, nor that there is any hell.
>
> The second misfortune is that for three years no crops have been harvested. In the past year, 1668, a great many Indians perished of hunger, lying dead along the roads, in the ravines, and in their huts. There were pueblos (as instance Humanas) where more than four hundred and fifty died of hunger. The same calamity still prevails, for, because of lack of money, there is not a fanega of corn or of wheat in the whole kingdom, so that for two years the food of Spaniards, men and women alike, has been the hides of cattle which they had in their houses. To make them edible they toast them, and then eat them. And the great misfortune of all is that they can no longer find a bit of leather to eat, for their herds are dying.

A second document, this one from 1679, provided additional details of the problems of the early 1670s:

> [I]n the year 1670 there was a very great famine in those provinces, which compelled the Spanish inhabitants and the Indians alike to eat the hides that they had and the straps of the carts, preparing them for food by soaking and washing them and toasting them in the fire with maize, and boiling them with herbs and roots. By this means almost half the people in the said provinces escaped [starvation]. There followed in the next year

THE DEMISE OF THE INDIAN POPULATIONS   111

of 1671 a great pestilence which also carried off many people and cattle; and shortly thereafter, in the year of 1672, the hostile Apaches who were then at peace rebelled and rose up, and the said province was totally sacked and robbed by their attacks and outrages, especially of all the cattle and sheep, of which it had previously been very productive. They killed, stole, and carried off all except a few small flocks of sheep which were saved by the vigilance and care of some of the inhabitants, who guarded them by day at great risk of losing their lives, as some did, and locked them up at night in the patios and corrals of their own houses.

Famine, disease, and attacks by hostile Indians, Apaches as well as rebel Pueblos, made it extremely difficult to continue to occupy the now vulnerable Salinas province, and it was abandoned before the outbreak of the Pueblo revolt in 1680.

The abandonment of the Salinas province apparently occurred in several stages. First, the Franciscans and pueblos abandoned the southern Pueblos including Humanas, Abo, and Quarai. Quarai apparently was the first abandoned, and the inhabitants of the Pueblo moved to Tajique in 1676 or 1677. Before the outbreak of the revolt in 1680, the inhabitants of the last Salinas pueblos abandoned their communities and moved to the Rio Grande Valley pueblos such as Ysleta. Hundreds of the Pueblo Indians from Salinas province followed the Spanish out of New Mexico in 1680 and settled in new communities in the El Paso area such as Ysleta del Sur.

Pecos, also located on the eastern frontier of New Mexico, serves as a case study of population decline in the New Mexico pueblos. As was the case in Salinas province discussed above, hostile Indians raided Pecos, contributing to the decline of the population. Pecos was also the site of a trade fair, and its population fluctuated, but generally dropped during the course of the seventeenth and eighteenth centuries. In the 1620s, some 2,000 people inhabited Pecos; in 1706 there were 1,000 following the Spanish reoccupation of the province. The numbers experienced a steady decline from that point. There were 521 in 1730, 344 in 1760, 123 in 1800, and a mere 18 in 1838 when the Indians abandoned the pueblo. The decline certainly was related to epidemic and endemic disease, although gaps and under-registration in the surviving sacramental registers prevent an accurate evaluation of patterns of fertility and mortality. There was also out-migration from the community, as residents of the pueblo moved to the pueblos located on the Rio Grande that were not as exposed to raids. At the same time the settler population of the

Pecos Valley grew. There were 735 *vecinos* in 1821, and 1,519 in 1845 shortly before the American conquest of New Mexico. Unlike the pueblos located in the Rio Grande Valley, the population of Pecos did not recover at the end of the colonial period, but this continued demographic stagnation and decline was related as much to the uncertainty wrought by raids as to the effects of disease.

Race and Status in the Indigenous Population

The Spanish historically defined social status and identity on the basis of birth and blood lines. Iberia evolved during the Middle Ages as a multi-ethnic society also divided along religious lines. These divisions found a larger context in the crusader ethic of the *reconquista*, the reconquest or liberation of most of Iberia from the Muslims, who had occupied most of the peninsula in the eighth century. These elements bread intolerance and a preoccupation with blood lines that evolved into the doctrine of *limpieza de sangre* (purity of blood). Families that aspired to place a son or daughter in government service or the Catholic Church had to prove in a legal document that they descended from "old Christians" and did not have the taint of Jewish, Muslim, or African blood. The Spanish carried this preoccupation with limpieza de sangre to America, and in a new multi-ethnic society blood lines formed the basis of colonial social structure.

The Spanish created a series of caste terms based on both the preoccupation with blood lines and the assumption that parish priests, missionaries, and census takers could determine blood lines, and hence caste status, based on physical characteristics and skin color. The status and identity of the indigenous population fit into the larger context of the caste system, and the term *indio* defined a fiscal status. Individuals defined as indios shared certain stereotypical elements attributed to them by the Spaniards, and by law had to provide labor services and pay *tributo*, a poll tax paid only by the indigenous population. The native peoples of northern Mexico living on the missions generally did not have to pay tributo or provide labor services through a draft. The exceptions were the New Mexico *encomiendas* of the seventheeth century and the mining labor draft in parts of Sonora. The caste system evolved differently on the northern frontier, as typified by patterns that can be documented for Sonora.

The caste system and colonial institutions evolved very differently

THE DEMISE OF THE INDIAN POPULATIONS 113

on the frontier than in the core areas of Spanish America, where the objective of Spanish policymakers was to create separate corporate groups. On the frontier of New Spain, the goal of caste identification was to incorporate the indigenous populations into a new colonial order that, under the best conditions, would rely on the exploitation of labor and the collection of tribute. As a result of the temporary exemption from tribute of the indigenous populations living in the missions, tribute category terms did not appear in censuses and other records as they did in other parts of Spanish America. Indio status and the use of caste terms was imprecise and subjective, and, since the exploitation of indios through formal labor drafts and tribute collection did not figure as prominently in the frontier colonial system, precise definitions of caste status were not as important. Moreover, priests showed preferences in the use of specific terms, and some negotiation occurred over the choice of categories used to identify people, particularly in the marriage bans and marriage registers. Many indios renegotiated their status by seeking work on the mines and ranches, and in this way modified their behavior so as to not conform to the stereotypical elements that constituted indio status.

The caste system was not fully developed on the frontier, and to a certain extent the use of racial or, more commonly, ethnic terms to identify the indigenous populations served to differentiate between peoples living under Spanish rule and those who did not. Many priests did not use any of the conventional caste terms, or else used generic categories such as *vecino* (a member of a community with full rights to community resources such as land) or *gente de razón* ("people of reason") to describe the nonindigenous population. Priests and government officials used different tribal/ethnic terms to identify the indigenous populations to a greater extent, and since the tribute system did not function, fiscal terms derived from it did not appear in documents.

In the last decades of the eighteenth century some Sonora missionaries and parish priests did not use caste terms to define the status of newborn children. Ures missionary Joseph Medina, O.F.M., recorded only the status of local tribal peoples in the 1770s. On December 26, 1778, Medina baptized a newborn girl whom he simply identified as "de este Pueblo [from this village—Ures]." A week later, on January 2, 1779, Medina baptized another newborn girl he identified as both a "Hiaqui" and "una india de aquí de este Pueblo" [an Indian from this village]. Four days later, on January 6, 1779, Medina baptized a third newborn girl he identified as "una india de Santa Rosalia [an Indian from Santa

Rosalia]." In contrast, the missionaries stationed at Sahuaripa in the same years consistently assigned a racial status to newborn children.

Two related demographic trends occurred at Sahuaripa and surrounding communities within the jurisdiction of Sahuaripa. The first was the decline in the Opata population from an estimated contact population in the Sahuaripa Valley of some 8,750 to some 461 in the mid-1760s. The second was the establishment of mining camps and other settlements in the Sahuaripa Valley and surrounding valleys. The first mining strike was at Tacupeto in 1675, and over the next century there were other short-lived mining booms. In 1799, the settler population in the valley was 1,115, and the numbers grew to 1,255 in 1802, and 1,401 in 1806. Many settlers went to live in Sahuaripa and other mission communities. The remaining Indians were increasingly marginalized and in some instances lost control over the lands previously assigned to them.

Baptismal records for Sahuaripa survive for the years 1781 to 1856. However, in 1824, after the declaration of the first federal republic in Mexico, priests dropped the practice of recording racial terms in sacramental registers. As such, the analysis of patterns of assigning racial identity to newborn children is limited to the years 1781–1824. During these years four priests were stationed at Sahuaripa: Pedro de la Cueva (1781–1803); Ramon Mendieta (1803–1807); José Cuevas (1807–1813); and Dionisio Onederra (1814–1824). Each of the four priests showed a marked preference for specific racial terms recorded in the baptismal registers.

All four priests consistently categorized newborn indigenous children by one or another related term, such as *indio*. The frequency of newborns identified as indios ranged from 10 to 14 percent. The greatest variation occurred in the caste categories for the population of European and mixed ancestry. The frequency of the category *español* fluctuated from 19 to 38 percent. It was from 0 to 34 percent for the *mestizo* category, from 2 to 22 percent for the *mulato* (defined as mix of European and African) category, and from 9 to 35 percent for the *coyote* category. Pedro de la Cueva showed a preference for the mulato category, José Cuevas identified more children as coyotes, and Dionisio Onederra categorized children as mestizos and coyotes while at the same time making less use of the español category than had his predecessor Cuevas.

The general pattern that emerges, exclusive of cases such as Sahuaripa where the priests continued the categorization of the population based

THE DEMISE OF THE INDIAN POPULATIONS

on defining blood lines, was to first differentiate between the indigenous and nonindigenous populations, and then make distinctions between the indigenous groups under and outside of Spanish control such as Pimas and Apaches. Along these lines the Spanish created many pseudoethnic identities that distinguished between friendly and not so friendly indigenous groups. The use of these pseudoethnic categories also figures into an understanding of demographic patterns discussed earlier. While trying to collapse the Indian populations living at the missions into a single generic or pseudoethnic identity, the missionaries identified new converts as being different or distinct. This justified claims that the missionaries continued to make significant strides in reducing new groups to mission life, which proved useful when trying to fend off efforts to close down the missions. The stress placed on continued conversion was particularly important in light of the demographic decline of the indigenous populations living on the missions.

Chapter 6

The Demise of the Mission System

The mission system came under attack at the end of the eighteenth century as Spanish enlightened reformers questioned the paternalistic control that the missionaries exercised over the native converts. Some reformers advocated more integration of Indians into colonial society and the removal of Indians from the day-to-day control of the missionaries. As was the case in Sonora in the 1720s, the attack on the missions was also motivated by self-interest, since settlers hoped to gain native lands and labor. The expulsion of the Jesuits in 1767–1768 resulted in some experimentation with the mission system under the direction of José de Galvez, but ultimately the colonial government went back to the previous system of paternalistic control by the missionaries. Many of the calls for reform of the missions did not win favor with the Spanish government.

Decline of the indigenous populations also contributed to the demise of the mission system. Missionaries could justify their continued management of the missions as long as there were active congregations, meaning that there were recent converts still receiving religious instruction. Writings of Franciscans stationed in California clearly show that the missionaries were cognizant of the need to continue the resettlement of converts on the missions in order to justify their continued operation. On the other hand, the decline of the indigenous populations and the end of active congregation gave the government grounds for secularizing the missions. Secularization entailed the assumption of clerical duties by a member of the secular clergy, and the appointment of a lay administrator to manage the mission estates and/or the division of mission property among the surviving indigenous converts and in many instances local settlers.

The secularization of the San Antonio missions in Texas resulted from the decline of the indigenous population, coupled with local political considerations. The Spanish government first closed down San Antonio de Valero in 1794, to make former mission lands available to landless settlers who had lived in San Antonio. Most of these landless settlers had lived at San Antonio for several decades after having been removed from east Texas settlements following the abandonment of missions and military garrisons there in the early 1770s. At the time of the secularization of San Antonio mission only some fifteen indigenous families survived, and the indigenous heads of household also received plots from the lands of the former mission. The other four San Antonio area missions also experienced partial secularization with the appointment of secular administrators, but because of the shortage of secular priests in Texas, the Franciscans continued to serve as parish priests.

The early and mid-nineteenth century was the eve of liberal reform in Mexico. Liberalism challenged the ancien regime (neofeudal order) in an effort to modernize society and the economy along the lines of Great Britain and the United States. Liberal reformers challenged the notion of a corporate society where people were members of different groups that had distinct privileges and obligations to the government. A number of the corporate groups enjoyed judicial *fueros*, the right to a separate court to try all cases that involved members of the corporate group. Members of the new liberal society would be identified as individuals rather than as members of a corporate group, and there would be a level playing field where all, regardless of the station of their birth, would be able to advance upward based on their own abilities. The same body of law would govern members of society.

The liberals also stressed the development of an unencumbered economy free of laws that controlled or regulated the exchange of goods and services, and free of inheritance laws that kept real property out of the market. Liberals attacked *mayorazgo*, or entail—a suspension of the laws of partible inheritance that allowed elite families to keep their estates intact over generations—as well as ownership of urban real property and rural land by corporate groups such as charitable institutions (hospitals and orphanages), indigenous communities, and the Catholic Church. Liberals argued that corporate groups held real property in mortmain (dead hand)— the idea that rented properties would decline in productivity— and entail. This meant that corporate landowners did not sell their properties, and in the case of the Church and charitable institutions lived off the rents paid for the property and did not reinvest profits to increase production or productivity. Moreover, the renters had no interest in reinvesting or even maintaining the rented properties. As a result, there was long-term deterioration of the rental properties, and these properties would never enter the market and could not be sold to individuals who would increase production and productivity. In the case of the indigenous communities, it was commonly believed that community members did not have the intelligence or knowledge to improve their lands. The solution was to force corporate landowners to sell their lands, and make the indigenous community members take individual title to the plots of land they already exploited in usufruct.

Finally, the liberals challenged the role of the Catholic Church in society and the economy. The Church had historically been a bastion of the colonial order, and exercised a monopoly over education. If the liberals were to create a new society, they had to secularize education, which was so important as a vehicle of indoctrination, and have the government assume functions such as the registration of vital statistics that had been a Church monopoly. Liberals also believed that the Church controlled a significant amount of Mexican wealth and that this retarded economic development. In the 1830s, ideologue José Mora argued that the Church controlled somewhere between one-quarter and one-third of Mexico's wealth. Mora and other Mexican liberals also advocated the greater integration of the indigenous population into Mexican social and political life. They criticized the frontier missions because they were overly paternalistic and had actually prevented the indigenous population from assuming its role in society. Moreover, the missions controlled land and other resources that did not contribute to the economic development of the frontier.

In the nineteenth century the Spanish and later the newly independent Mexican governments took actions that eventually caused the demise of the missions. Between 1812 and 1814, the Spanish *cortes* (parliament) instituted liberal policies, including an 1813 law secularizing the missions in northern Mexico. King Ferdinand VII closed down the cortes in 1814 and reversed all of its legislative actions, including the 1813 secularization law. However, with Mexican independence in 1821, the days of the frontier mission were numbered.

The Mexican government took several actions that undermined the viability of the frontier missions. In the late 1820s the government expelled many Spaniards from the country, including Spanish-born missionaries. During the prolonged civil war (1810–1821) and in the immediate aftermath of independence, many Spaniards had already left Mexico, and by the mid-1820s the missionary orders (Franciscans, Dominicans) already faced difficulties in finding enough missionaries to staff the missions. A number of frontier missionaries had supported Spain during the civil war, and following independence refused to support, let alone acknowledge, the government of independent Mexico. The expulsion laws gutted the missions in areas already in decline such as Texas, northern Sonora, and Baja California, and made it difficult to find personnel for New Mexico. In California, on the other hand, the government exempted the Spanish-born Franciscans from expulsion. The Franciscans continued to congregate non-Christian natives to the missions, and the missionaries were allowed to remain. Nevertheless, the Apostolic College of San Fernando, the Franciscan entity that staffed and managed the California missions, found it difficult to recruit new personnel, and in 1833 allowed the rival Apostolic College of Zacatecas to assume responsibility for half of the California missions. In the same year a contingent of Mexican-born Franciscans arrived from Zacatecas to staff missions in California.

The second significant action was the passage in 1833 of a law secularizing the missions in northern Mexico. Liberals had come to power for a short period of time, and under the leadership of Valentín Gómez Farías passed many reform laws. At the time, Mexico was a federal republic modeled on the United States, and individual state/territorial governments assumed responsibility for implementation of mandates from Mexico City. Even after the fall of the liberals from power in 1834, the California territorial government continued to implement the secularization law. The missions in the other areas studied here were already moribund because of their small surviving populations coupled with the shortage of missionaries. It was only in California that the secularization law destroyed a still functioning system.

As implemented in California, the secularization law entailed the appointment of a civil administrator to administer the mission estates. The Franciscans remained as parish priests, but no longer enjoyed day-to-day control over the lives of the converts or of the mission estates. Secularization did not mean immediate emancipation of the natives living on the missions, many of whom remained under the control of the civil administrators. The intent of the mission program was to prepare the indigenous converts to live in autonomous corporate communities, but as the civil administrators assumed control over the missions they deemed many natives not ready for emancipation.

Prior to secularization there had been several experiments in emancipation of the natives living on the missions. In 1826, the government emancipated more acculturated natives living in the missions in southern and central California. The Franciscans complained that the emancipated natives no longer performed work at the missions, and that many had migrated to the emerging towns in the province. Between 1825 and 1830, there was an exodus, and the number of Indians living on seven nonmission settlements increased from 154 to 427. A second emancipation occurred in May of 1833, and included an effort to create an autonomous indigenous community at San Juan Capistrano mission. Ultimately the newly created *pueblo de indios* failed because of exploitation by the civil administrator of the mission and the dissipation of former mission property. Many abandoned the pueblo de indios. The bulk of the indigenous population living on the ex-missions remained under the control of the administrators until finally emancipated in 1840, although there was also a mass exodus from the missions after 1834. Something like 60 percent of the natives living on the missions in 1834 left over the next eight years. The Indians that left went to work on emerging ranches and towns, or back into the interior of the province beyond Mexican control.

The civil administrators also presided over the dispersion of the accumulated wealth of the mission estates, particularly land and livestock. The administration of the mission estates operated under contradictory government policy. Colonization laws passed in the early 1820s that intended to promote settlement of the frontier gave governors authority to make grants of land. In California the most attractive lands were the former mission lands, and between 1834 and 1846 California governors made more than 800 land grants. Recipients of land grants also tapped existing herds of former mission livestock. Administrators personally benefited from their jobs, but they also loaned or sold animals to other prominent settlers to start herds on newly acquired ranches. The greatest depletion of livestock occurred with the herds of cattle and flocks of mission sheep (see figure 6.1). The mission administrators ordered the slaughter of cattle for hides and tallow (rendered fat) for export. The hides were shipped, for example, to New England shoe factories, and tallow was the base material for the manufacture of soap and candles.

The Franciscans had overseen the development of ranching and farm-

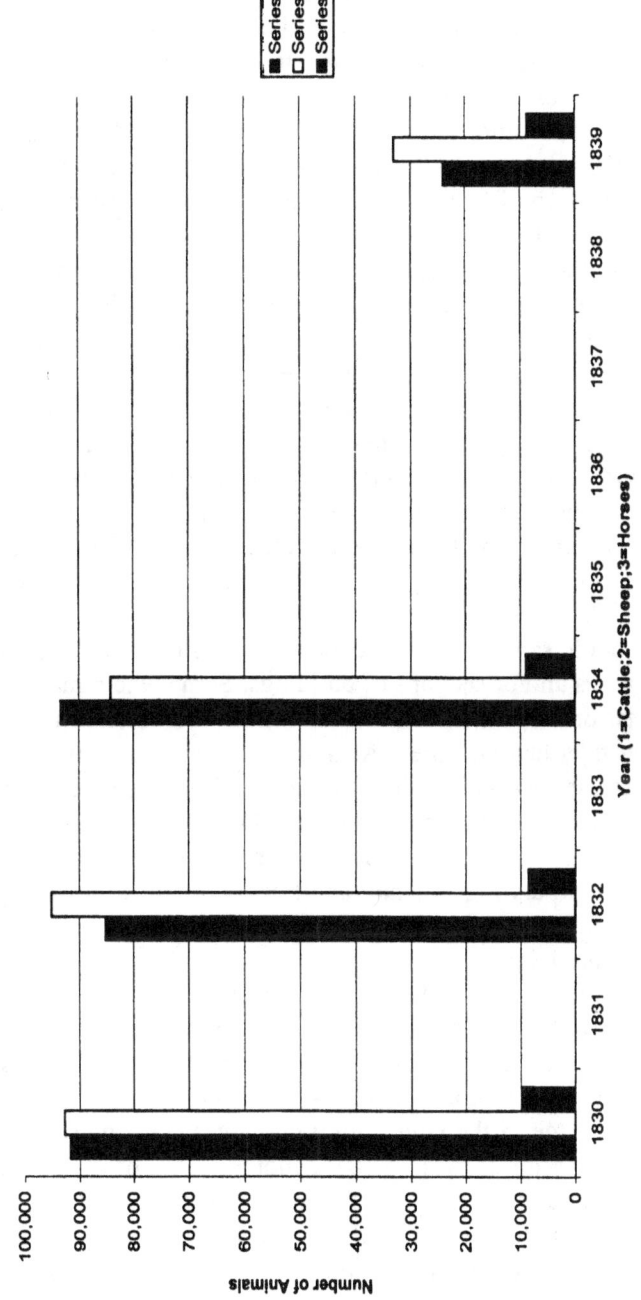

Figure 6.1 Cattle, Sheep, and Horses Reported at Thirteen California Missions, 1830–1839

Source: Data compiled from Robert H. Jackson and Edward Castillo, *Indians, Franciscans and Spanish Colonialization: The Impact of the Mission System on California Indians*. Albuquerque: University of New Mexico, 1995, 101–102.

ing stations at different spots within the extensive grants of land assigned to each mission, and these developed sites were very attractive to settlers applying for land grants under the colonization laws. One case, that of Rancho Paso de Robles, demonstrates the attraction of the developed ranches. Paso de Robles was a farming out-station of San Miguel mission developed after 1800 with the construction of buildings including a large granary. An 1839 census of San Miguel mission reported a sizable population of 190 Indians at Paso de Robles growing wheat and barley. In contrast, only 112 converts continued to live at the main mission village. Paso de Robles and other ranches and farming stations of San Miguel mission formed the nucleus of private ranches, but the Indians still living at the mission and out-stations protested the alienation of land, livestock, buildings, and equipment they believed rightfully belonged to them. When granted to a non-Indian applicant, Rancho Paso de Robles embraced an area of nearly 26,000 acres, including the developed farming station with the large indigenous population living there. The 1839 report on the state of the former mission, prepared for the local government by William Hartnell, recorded a number of such complaints by Indians still living on the former missions, but these fell on deaf ears.

This is not to say that no indigenous residents of the former missions received lands and/or sections of buildings. Some who remained at the former mission long enough did receive small plots of land and the apartments that they had occupied. At Santa Cruz mission, for example, a group of former neophytes received a plot of land that they worked in common. They held the land until the 1840s, when incoming Anglo-American settlers bought them out. Similarly, a number of families received rooms in a wing of small apartments that had previously been assigned to indigenous families. The owners of the apartments sold their rights to nonindigenous settlers.

The granting of lands and culling of the herds of former mission livestock rapidly depleted the value of the mission estates built up under the direction of the Franciscan missionaries. One of the first actions taken by the newly appointed civil administrators was to take inventory and estimate the value of the lands, buildings, livestock, and so forth, that made up the mission estates. In 1845, another series of inventories was prepared, recording the value of the mission estates in anticipation of their possible sale by local officials. The new inventories documented a considerable drop in the value of the mission estates. A comparison of

123

Figure 6.2 Value of Selected California Mission Estates, 1834/35 and 1845

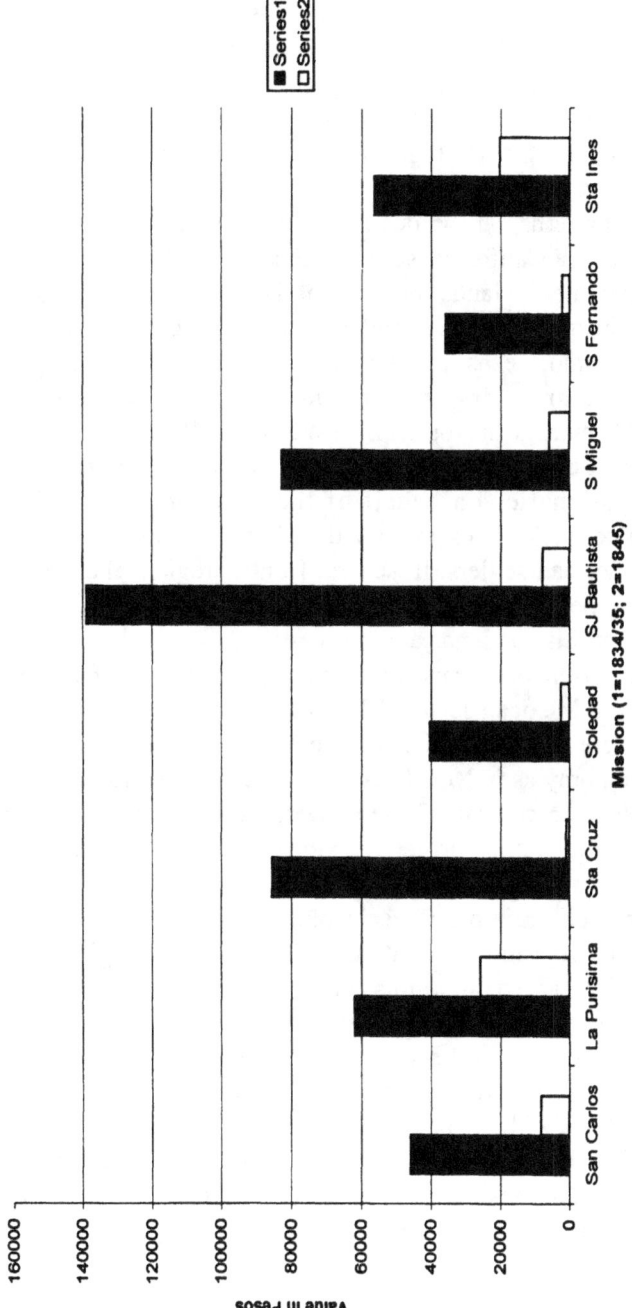

Source: Data compiled from Robert H. Jackson and Edward Castillo, *Indians, Franciscans and Spanish Colonialization: The Impact of the Mission System on California Indians*. Albuquerque: University of New Mexico, 1995, 99.

the value of eight mission estates shows a decline from some 548,110 pesos in 1834–1835 to 73,755 pesos in 1845 (see figure 6.2). The erosion of the value of the mission estates was already apparent when William Hartnell prepared his 1839 report on the condition of the recently secularized missions. As noted above, the number of livestock was already down, and Indians registered complaints about the alienation of land and other mission property.

Similar patterns can be documented for other regions in northern Mexico. In Baja California, settlers and retired soldiers created ranches from former mission lands and herds of livestock. Similarly, many prime parcels of irrigated farmland and sections of the building complexes of the San Antonio, Texas, missions passed into the hands of prominent local settlers, including in some instances the civil administrators appointed to manage the former missions. In the 1830s and 1840s, settlers in northern Sonora began to file claims to lands previously claimed by the missionaries on behalf of the Pima population. The New Mexico Pueblos also experienced land disputes with Mexican and Anglo-American settlers. In several frontier regions the demographic collapse of the indigenous populations made it easier for settlers to acquire former mission lands and property.

Did the closure of the missions hasten the integration of native peoples into northern Mexican society? To a limited extent, yes, although most converts were marginalized, and in some instances either retained communal autonomy as in New Mexico or else returned to life beyond the pale of Mexican control. Those converts who continued to live in the neighborhood of the former missions in Texas, Sonora, and Baja California retained some lands, and also constituted a lower-class laboring group. California offers very complex patterns. As already noted, some former mission residents migrated to the emerging towns and ranches being carved out of mission and public domain lands. An 1836 census of Monterey and surrounding districts already showed the presence of some Indian workers on the recently created ranches, as well as Indian servants working in the town itself. The natives became an underclass that, with the passage of time, was denigrated and despised. Many natives left the coastal territory dominated by the Mexicans, and either returned to the interior or else went to work on the Russian farms north of San Francisco Bay. In this way they escaped Mexican control entirely.

On balance, the lofty goal of preparing the indigenous population for a role in a new society must be considered a failure. Contradictory government policies within a federal political system allowed prominent settlers to acquire much of the property acquired and developed under the direction of the missionaries. The demographic collapse of the indigenous populations undermined the acculturation campaign, and many of the survivors chose to not remain under the Mexican sphere of control. Those who did so increasingly found themselves marginalized and prevented from attaining the benefits of their labors, and following the conquest of northern Mexico by the United States these natives became a part of a despised non-Anglo population. Many Mexican settlers and Indians only came to the attention of the new dominant society through reports of criminal behavior, but otherwise faded away from sight to the margins of Anglo society.

Chapter 7

Conclusions

Several questions can be asked regarding the legacy of the frontier missions in northern Mexico. By the criteria established by the Spanish government, the missions failed to create stable indigenous communities, except in New Mexico where the population already lived in permanent villages and practiced agriculture. The populations of all of the frontier missions experienced drastic declines in numbers, and demographic collapse undermined the goal of creating Catholic villagers. However, not all indigenous populations disappeared. The native population of New Mexico stabilized and later recovered in the nineteenth century after serious losses in the seventeenth and eighteenth centuries. In another sense, though, the mission system did help the Spanish government colonize and control frontier regions that otherwise might not have had resources attractive to nonindigenous settlers.

With the exception of New Mexico, most mission populations declined, and following the closing of the missions either dispersed or continued to live in the vicinity of the former missions. In northern Sonora, some surviving natives continued to reside at the mission villages, although settlers began to claim former mission lands and settled on the mission villages themselves. The few surviving Coahuiltecans settled on the San Antonio area missions in Texas lived on former mission lands, but in the minds of the Anglo-Americans who settled in the city after the 1830s they blended in with the larger Mexican population.

Few natives remained in Baja California, except for the northern frontier along the Pacific Coast known as La Frontera. However, the population of the missions dropped after about 1800 as the number of new converts declined. In the 1820s and 1830s few Dominican missionaries remained, and several Indian revolts forced the last missionary to flee the region. Well into the twentieth century a large community of Indians lived at Santa Catalina, the site of one of the Dominican missions destroyed in an uprising in 1834.

Sizeable numbers of Indians survived in Alta California following the closing of the missions, although, as noted in the previous chapter, large numbers left the area of effective Mexican control along the coast. Many remained in the proximity of the former missions, and in the eyes of Anglo-Americans also blended in with the Mexican population. During most of the nineteenth century Indian rancherías existed on the margins of Anglo-American towns or in some instances close to the former mission building complexes, and occasionally an Indian made it into the Anglo press. There are some bizarre examples of this, such as the competition between Santa Cruz and Monterey to have the oldest living Indian. Boosters of Santa Cruz advertised Justiniano Rojas as being the oldest man on earth, based on a misreading of mission records by the parish priest stationed at the Catholic church built on the site of the mission. A recent study of mission sacramental records shows that Justiniano Rojas and the rest of his family died off years before the newly christened Justiniano Rojas appeared on the scene.

Indians also appeared in the consciousness of California Anglo society through well-publicized criminal proceedings. One such case occurred in Ventura in 1881. Chumash Indian Vicente García received the death penalty, later commuted to life imprisonment, for the murder of Estanislao, another Chumash Indian. Before he died, Estanislao identified Vicente García, Jesús Sosa, and an unidentified third man as his attackers. The crime took place in the lower west end of Ventura, known as "Indian Town" (in 1880, forty-six Chumash lived in Ventura). García and two others were tried for murder in highly publicized proceedings, and García was found guilty in a speedy trial that lasted only one day. García did not receive a fair trial, and the judge denied a postponement that would have allowed a key defense witness to appear. Much of the prosecution's case relied on the evidence of a very unreliable witness who presented contradictory accounts and had been named by Estanislao as one of his attackers. García spent the rest of his life in prison at San Quentin, where he died in 1899. Efforts at obtaining a new trial failed, as did a request for a pardon. In fact, rates of pardons for Indian prisoners in late nineteenth-century California were the lowest for all ethnic groups in the state.

The mission system was by all accounts the most important colonial institution on the frontier of northern Mexico. Its historical legacy and the effects of Spanish colonization continue to be explored by scholars, and constitute a very controversial and in some regards a high-stakes issue. This can be seen in the ongoing campaign to canonize Father Junipero Serra, the architect of the California mission system and the signatory to the agreement with the colonial government in Mexico City to supply the presidios. Advocates of canonization led by the vice postulator for the Serra cause, Father Noel Moholy, O.F.M. have presented a highly sanitized version of mission history in order to appeal to the hearts, minds, and pocketbooks of pious Californians. In arguing their case, however, the canonization boosters presented an ahistorical and highly biased view of the missions and indigenous culture. The Serra canonization boosters have not included the descendants of the indigenous residents of the missions in their campaign, and in one instance actually excluded native peoples: In the late 1980s Pope John Paul II visited San Carlos mission, where Serra is buried. Descendants of the indigenous population that had inhabited San Carlos mission were kept at some distance from the pope, while thousands of nonindigenous Catholics were bused in to San Carlos mission and a nearby race track where the pope conducted an open air mass.

In 1984, the bishop of Monterey prepared a press release entitled "The Serra Report." In it, a number of scholars who support canonization presented their views of the Franciscans, the missions, and native society. The major theme of the report was taken from the older church self-history triumphalism, and stressed that the Franciscans brought civilization and religion to the savage Indians. One contributor, historian Doyce Nunis, in response to the question "What Did This Religion Do for the Indians?" noted that:

> For the first time it dignified the individual. Up until that time, the Indians had no sense of fidelity to each other, there was no spirit of loyalty. There was no spirit of commitment. You stayed together out of necessity rather than out of appreciation. In other words, they had no idea of a social compact, in the strongest sense of the word. . . . They had no sense of morality. They participated in free love.

CONCLUSIONS

The previous chapters have illuminated, I hope, the complexity of the mission system on the northern frontier of Mexico. The mission was a government-funded institution that served the ends of colonial policy, and the Indians who lived on the missions or refused to accept mission life were active participants in the history of that institution. Some natives reached accommodation with the Franciscans, while others resisted. However, their role and their fate cannot be forgotten.

Bibliographic Essay

The purpose of this bibliographic essay is to provide an introduction to selected sources relevant to the study of the missions of northern Mexico. I will list selected publications along thematic lines. The first theme is what I have called Church self-history.

The Jesuit Peter Dunne wrote a series of narrative studies of the Jesuit mission program in Sinaloa, Sonora, Baja California, and the Tarahumara region of Chihuahua. See, for example, his *Pioneer Black Robes on the West Coast* (Berkeley and LosAngeles 1940) and *Black Robes in Lower California* (Berkeley and Los Angeles, 1952). Two other Jesuits wrote histories of Jesuit missions on the frontier of northern Mexico: John Bannon authored *The Mission Frontier in Sonora, 1620–1687* (New York, 1955); John Donohue wrote *After Kino: Jesuit Missions in Northwestern New Spain 1711–1767* (Rome and St. Louis, 1969).

Franciscans have also written histories of Franciscan missions. For Texas, see Marion Habig, O.F.M., *The Alamo Chain of Missions* (Chicago, 1968). Zephyrin Engelhardt, O.F.M., was the most prolific author of histories of the Franciscan missions. He wrote a four-volume series entitled *Missions and Missionaries of California* (San Francisco, 1908). He also wrote histories of individual missions in California, although prior to his death in 1933 he had not completed histories of all twenty-one California missions. Not all Franciscan historians have written studies that can be considered biased Church self-history. For an example of a more balanced and well-documented study written by a Franciscan see Kieran McCarty, O.F.M., *A Spanish Frontier in the Enlightened Age: Franciscan Beginnings in Sonora and Arizona, 1767–1770* (Washington, DC, 1981).

Ethnography/ethnohistory—the study of indigenous culture, society, and religion—is very important for the study of the frontier missions. The magisterial *Handbook of North American Indians*, published by the

Smithsonian Institution Press, is the basic source to consult. Volume 4 (1990) focuses on Indian-European relations; volume 8 (1978) documents the indigenous population of California; volumes 9 (1988) and 10 (1983) discuss the native peoples of the Southwest and northern Mexico. An example of an older ethnology based on field work is Campbell Pennington's, *The Pima Bajo of Central Sonora, Mexico*, 2 vols. (Salt Lake City, 1980). Anthropological/ethnohistorical approaches provided important perspectives that reversed the biased vision of Church self-historians. Edward Spicer wrote a sweeping volume entitled *Cycles of Conquest: The Impact of Spain, Mexico, and the United States on the Indians of the Southwest, 1533–1960* (Tucson, 1962), which covered indigenous responses to Spanish, Mexican, and Anglo-American intrusions into the Southwest. In his own field work Spicer studied the Yaqui of southern Sonora and the Tucson, Arizona area, and later wrote *The Yaquis: A Cultural History* (Tucson, 1980), which skillfully blended anthropological and historical perspectives. Archaeologists have added the study of material culture to the ethnohistorical approach; a fine example is Robert Ricklis, *The Karankawa Indians of Texas: An Ecological Study of Cultural Tradition and Change* (Austin, 1996).

Historical geographers trained at the University of California, Berkeley, by Carl Sauer completed detailed and for the time innovative studies of missions in Baja California that combined an economic, ecological, and demographic perspective. Peveril Meigs was the first of these geographers. In 1927, he coauthored with Sauer a study of a Franciscan mission on the peninsula titled "Site and Culture at San Fernando de Velicata," *University of California Publications in Geography* 2 (9): 271–303. Meigs went on to write a longer study of Dominican missions in the peninsula titled *The Dominican Mission Frontier of Lower California* (Berkeley, 1935). Homer Aschmann, also a Sauer student, authored "The Central Desert of Baja California: Demography and Ecology," *Ibero-Americana* 42 (1959).

One hotly debated issue has been the causes of the demographic decline and in some instances collapse of the indigenous populations of northern Mexico. Sherburne Cook was one of the first scholars to systematically explore the causes and manifestations of demographic decline. In the early 1940s Cook published a series of seminal monographs republished under the title *The Conflict Between the California Indian and White Civilization* (Berkeley and Los Angeles, 1976). In the same year the University of California Press published a collection of Cook's essays entitled *The Population of the California Indians 1769–1970* (Berkeley and Los Angeles, 1976). Cook established a long working relationship with historian Woodrow Borah that culminated in a three-volume series, *Essays in Population History* (Berkeley and Los Angeles, 1971–1979). Volume three contains an essay on demographic patterns in eight California missions. Mexican scholars have also studied demographic patterns in the missions. Mario Magana recently published a monograph titled *Población y misiones de Baja California* (Tijuana, 1998).

Other scholars have examined the question of population decline. Henry Dobyns published several provocative monographs, including *Spanish Colonial Tucson: A Demographic History* (Tucson, 1976) and *Their Numbers Become Thinned: Native American Population Dynamics in Eastern North America* (Knoxville, 1983). Dobyns has engaged other scholars in a debate over the size of the indigenous population at first contact, a debate that I refer to as "the numbers game." A number of studies have attempted to make reasonable estimates of contact population size, but in the end the result is an estimate that for different reasons can be criticized. Anthropologist Daniel Reff authored a study of culture change and the effects of epidemic disease on the native populations of Sonora: *Disease, Depopulation, and Culture Change in Northwestern New Spain, 1518–1764* (Salt Lake City, 1991).

My own scholarly contributions include studies of indigenous demographics in the missions as related to mission economics. I have authored, coauthored, edited, and coedited the following books relevant to the study of the frontier missions of northern Mexico: *Indian Demographic Collapse: The Missions of Northwestern New Spain, 1687–1840* (Albuquerque, 1994); Robert H. Jackson and Edward Castillo, *Indians, Franciscans, and Spanish Colonization: The Impact of the Mission System on California Indians* (Albuquerque, 1995); Erick Langer and Robert Jackson, editors, *The New Latin American Mission History* (Lincoln, 1995); and Robert H. Jackson, editor, *New Views of Borderlands History* (Albuquerque, 1998). The following journal articles also directly deal with the development of frontier missions: "Epidemic Disease and Indian Depopulation in the Baja California Missions, 1697–1834," *Southern California Quarterly* 63 (1981): 308–346; "The Last Jesuit Censuses of the Pimeria Alta Missions, 1761 and 1766," *The Kiva* 46 (1981): 243–272; "Causes of Indian Depopulation in the Pimeria Alta Missions of Northern Sonora," *Journal of Arizona History* 24 (1983): 405–429; "Demographic Patterns in the Missions of Northern Baja California,"

Journal of California and Great Basin Anthropology 5 (1983): 130–139; "Disease and Demographic Patterns at Santa Cruz Mission, Alta California," *Journal of California and Great Basin Anthropology* 5 (1983): 33–57; "Demographic Patterns in the Missions of Central Baja California," *Journal of California and Great Basin Anthropology* 6 (1984): 91–112; "Demographic Change in Northwestern New Spain," *The Americas* 41 (1985): 462–479 and reproduced in Antonine Tibesar, O.F.M., editor, *Junipero Serra and the Northwestern Mexican Frontier, 1750–1825* (Washington, DC, 1985); "Gentile Recruitment and Population Movements in the San Francisco Bay Area Missions," *Journal of California and Great Basin Anthropology* 6 (1984): 225–239; Robert H. Jackson and Peter Stern, "Vagabundaje and Settlement Patterns in Colonial Northern Sonora," *The Americas* 44 (1988): 461–481; Robert Jackson and Erick Langer, "Colonial and Republican Missions Compared: The Cases of Alta California and Southeastern Bolivia," *Comparative Studies in Society and History* 30 (1988): 286–311; "Patterns of Demographic Change in the Missions of Southern Baja California," *Journal of California and Great Basin Anthropology* 8 (1986): 273–279; "Patterns of Demographic Change in the Missions of Central Alta California," *Journal of California and Great Basin Anthropology* 9 (1987): 251–272; "The 1781–1782 Smallpox Epidemic in the Baja California Missions," *Journal of California and Great Basin Anthropology* 3 (1981): 138–143; "Intermarriage at Fort Ross: A Case from San Rafael Mission," *Journal of California and Great Basin Anthropology* 5 (1983): 240–241; "La dinámica del desastre demográfico de la población india en las misiones de la bahía de San Francisco, Alta California," *Historia Mexicana* 40 (1990): 187–215—an English-language version of this article was published in *American Indian Quarterly* 17 (Spring 1992): 141–156; "La colonización de la Alta California: Un análisis del desarrollo de dos comunidades misionales," *Historia Mexicana* 41 (1991): 83–110; "Population and the Economic Dimension of Colonization in Alta California: Four Mission Communities," *Journal of the Southwest* 33 (1991): 387–439; "The Dynamics of Indian Demographic Collapse in the Mission Communities of Northwestern New Spain: A Comparative Approach with Implications for Popular Interpretations of Mission History," in Virginia Guedea and Jaime Rodríguez O., editors, *Five Centuries of Mexican History/Cinco Siglos de Historia de Mexico*, 2 vols. (Mexico, D.F., 1992), vol. 1, 139–156; "The Changing Economic Structure of the Alta California Missions: A Reinterpretation," *Pacific His-*

torical Review 61:3 (1992): 387–415; "The Population of the Santa Barbara Channel Missions (Alta California), 1813–1832," *Journal of California and Great Basin Anthropology* 12:2 (1990): 268–274; "Patterns of Demographic Change in the Alta California Missions: The Case of Santa Inés," *California History* 71:3 (Fall 1992): 362–369; "The Impact of Liberal Policy on Mexico's Northern Frontier: Mission Secularization and the Development of Alta California, 1812–1846," *Colonial Latin American Historical Review* 2:2 (1993): 195–225; "Congregation and Population Change in the Mission Communities of Northern New Spain: Cases from the Californias and Texas," *New Mexico Historical Review* (April 1994): 163–183; "Grain Supply, Congregation, and Demographic Patterns in the Missions of Northwestern New Spain: Case Studies from Baja and Alta California," *Journal of the West* 34:1 (1997): 19–25.

A handful of scholars have published detailed studies of individual missions or groups of missions that reflect recent trends in the study of history. John Kessell authored three important narrative histories of individual frontier missions. The first two related to the northern Sonora frontier: *Mission of Sorrows: Jesuit Guevavi and the Pimas, 1691–1767* (Tucson, 1970); *Friars, Soldiers, and Reformers: Hispanic Arizona and the Sonora Mission Frontier 1767–1856* (Tucson, 1976). He later wrote a history of Pecos Pueblo in New Mexico titled *Kiva, Cross, and Crown: The Pecos Indians and New Mexico 1540–1840* (Washington, DC, 1979). At about the same time Elizabeth John published her detailed narrative history of Spanish-Indian relations in the Southwest titled *Storms Brewed in Other Men's Worlds: The Confrontation of Indians, Spanish, and French in the Southwest, 1540–1795* (College Station, 1975). Two books published in the 1990s and inspired by the postmodernism that has influenced historians, have also generated considerable controversy as well. Ramón Gutiérrez authored perhaps the most controversial book titled *When Jesus Came, the Corn Mothers Went Away: Marriage, Sexuality, and Power in New Mexico, 1500–1846* (Stanford, 1991). Gutiérrez challenged many established views of Pueblo society and the nature of Spanish-Indian relations. More recently a book by Cynthia Radding titled *Wandering Peoples: Colonialism, Ethnic Spaces, and Ecological Frontiers in Northwestern Mexico, 1700–1850* (Durham, 1997) tries to present a revisionistic social history of colonial Sonora, but often makes broad generalizations based on weak or incomplete evidence.

A number of sources document patterns of indigenous resistance to the Spanish. For New Mexico, *The Handbook of North American Indi-*

ans, vol. 9, contains essays on Spanish-Pueblo relations and the 1680 Pueblo revolt. The most complete source of primary documents available is Charmion Shelby, trans., and Charles Hackett, ed., *Revolt of the Pueblo Indians of New Mexico and Otermin's Attempted Reconquest 1680–1682*, 2 vols. (Albuquerque, 1942). There have been several synthetic histories of the Pueblo revolt, including Franklin Folsom, Indian *Uprising on the Rio Grande: The Pueblo Revolt of 1680*, reprint edition (Albuquerque, 1997).

The most important indigenous resistance in Baja California was the 1734–1737 uprising in the southern part of the peninsula. There are two important sources that document the uprising. The first is an article by Irving Leonard documenting an attack on the Manila galleon by rebels: "An Attempted Indian Attack on the Manila Galleon," *Hispanic American Historical Review* 11 (1931): 69–76. The second is an account of the uprising penned by one of the survivors of the revolt: Sigismundo Taraval, S.J., *The Indian Uprising in Lower California 1734–1737*, ed. and trans. Marguerite Eyer Wilbur (Los Angeles, 1931). Published primary sources, missionary letters, or mission histories also contain information on native resistance. See, for example, Juan María Salvatierra, S.J., *Selected Letters About Lower California*, trans. and ed. Ernest Burrus, S.J. (Los Angeles, 1971); Francisco Clavigero, S.J., *The History of California*, trans. and ed. Sara Lake and A.A. Gray (Palo Alto, 1937); Miguel del Barco, S.J., *Historia natural y crónica de la antigua California*, ed. Miguel León-Portilla (Mexico City, 1973); Johann Baegert, S.J., *Observations in Lower California*, trans. and ed. M. M. Brandenburg and Carl Baumann (Berkeley and Los Angeles, 1952); Homer Aschmann, trans. and ed., *The Natural and Human History of Baja California from Manuscripts by Jesuit Missionaries* (Los Angeles, 1966); Wenceslao Linck, S.J., *Reports and Letters 1762–1778*, trans. and ed. Earnest Burrus, S.J. (Los Angeles, 1967); Francisco Palou, O.F.M., *Historical Memoirs of New California*, 4 vols, trans. and ed. H. E. Bolton (New York, 1966); Luis Sales, O.P., *Observations on California*, trans. and ed. Charles Rudkin (Los Angeles, 1956); and Manuel Rojo, *Historical Notes on Lower California* (Los Angeles, 1971). Edward Castillo has documented native resistance to the Spanish in California in a series of publications. The most important is a compilation of previously published articles edited by Castillo entitled *Native American Perspectives on the Hispanic Colonization of California* (New York and London, 1991).

A discussion of indigenous resistance in Sonora includes raids by hostile groups living on the fringes of Spanish settlement and resistance by groups under Spanish rule. Sources on raiding by hostile Indians and Spanish responses to those raids include Joseph Parks, "Spanish Indian Policy in Northern Mexico, 1765–1810," *Arizona and the West* 4 (1962); Robert Stevens, "The Apache Menace in Sonora 1831–1849," *Arizona and the West* 6 (1964); Sidney Brinckerhoff, "The Last Years of Spanish Arizona 1786–1821," *Arizona and the West* 9 (1967); Thomas Sheridan, "Cross or Arrow? The Breakdown in Spanish–Seri Relations, 1729–1750," *Arizona and the West* 21 (1979); and María Soledad Arbeláez, "The Sonora Missions and Indian Raids of the Eighteenth Century," *Journal of the Southwest* 33 (1991). The most comprehensive discussion of late eighteenth-century Spanish-Apache relations all along the frontier is Max Moorhead, *The Apache Frontier: Jacobo Ugarte and Spanish-Indian Relations in Northern New Spain, 1769–1791* (Norman, 1968). There were several major rebellions by groups brought to live on the missions. The Yaqui rebellion of 1740 was the subject of a monograph written by Luis Navarro García and titled *La sublevación yaqui de 1740* (Sevilla, 1966). Russell Ewing pioneered the study of northern Pima resistance in a Ph.D. dissertation at the University of California-Berkeley, later summarized as "The Pima Revolt of 1751," in *Greater America: Essays in Honor of Herbert Eugene Bolton* (Berkeley, 1945).

The discussion of social and cultural change among the native peoples congregated in the missions relies largely on accounts by missionaries, many already referenced in this essay. There is a rich literature on evangelization in other parts of Spanish America. The classic statement of evangelization in central Mexico is Robert Ricard, *The Spiritual Conquest of Mexico: An Essay on the Apostolate and the Evangelization Methods of the Mendicant Orders in New Spain, 1523–1572*, trans. and ed. Lesley Byrd Simpson (Berkeley and Los Angeles, 1966). Recent studies have explored the question of religious conversion from the basis of a clearer understanding of native religion and the ways in which the indigenous populations responded to evangelization. Examples of this newer approach include Nancy Farriss, *Maya Society Under Colonial Rule: The Collective Enterprise of Survival* (Princeton, 1984); Fernando Cervantes, *The Devil in the New World: The Impact of Diabolism in New Spain* (New Haven, 1994); Sabine MacCormack, *Religion in the Andes: Vision and Imagination in Early Colonial Peru* (Princeton, 1991); Nicholas Griffiths, *The Cross and the Serpent: Religious Repression and Resurgence in Colonial Peru* (Norman, 1996).

In many areas in northern Mexico Spanish settlers lived close to the missions and contributed to the process of indigenous social and cultural change in both positive and negative ways. For an overview of Spanish settlement on the northern frontier, see Robert H. Jackon, "Repeopling the Land: The Spanish Borderlands," *Encyclopedia of North American Colonies*, 3 vols. (New York, 1993), vol. 2, 320–327. Examples of studies of nonindigenous settlement in northern Mexico include James Hastings, "People of Reason and Others: The Colonization of Sonora to 1767," *Arizona and the West*, 3 (1961): 321–340, and Jesús F. De la Teja, *San Antonio de Bexar: A Community on New Spain's Northern Frontier* (Albuquerque, 1995). Mobility on the frontier was an important aspect of social formation, but at the same time mobility caused consternation for royal official and missionary alike because of the instability of communities. A general study of frontier mobility is Michael Swann, *Migrants in the Mexican North: Mobility, Economy, and Society in a Colonial World* (Boulder, 1989). A more detailed examination of mobility and settlement patterns in Sonora is Peter Stern and Robert H. Jackson, "Vagabundaje and Settlement Patterns in Colonial Northern Sonora," *The Americas* 44 (1988): 461–481.

A discussion of society in Spanish America and the status of the native populations in the larger society should consider the question of race/caste status and identity. My own study, *Race, Caste, and Status: Indians in Colonial Spanish America* (Albuquerque, 1999), explores the questions of race/caste status and identity in two Spanish American regions, including the northern frontier of Mexico. The issue of race and status has concerned scholars for several decades. See, for example, Rodney Anderson, "Race and Social Stratification: A Comparison of Working Class Spaniards, Indians, and Castas in Guadalajara, Mexico in 1821," *The Hispanic American Historical Review* 68 (1988): 209–244; Adrian Bustamante, "The Matter Was Never Resolved: The Casta System in Colonial New Mexico, 1693–1823," *New Mexico Historical Review* 66 (1991): 143–164; John Chance, *Race and Class in Colonial Oaxaca* (Stanford, 1978); John Chance and William Taylor, "Estate and Class in a Colonial City: Oaxaca in 1792," *Comparative Studies in Society and History* 19 (1977): 454–487, and "Estate and Class: A Reply," *Comparative Studies in Society and History* 21 (1979), 343–442; Robert McCaa, "Calidad, Class, and Marriage in Colonial Mexico: The Case of Parral, 1788–1790," *The Hispanic American Historical Review* 64 (1984): 477–501; Robert McCaa, Stuart Schwartz, and Arturo

Grubessich, "Race and Class in Colonial Latin America: A Critique," *Comparative Studies in Society and History* 21 (1979): 421–433; Patricia Seed, "The Social Dimensions of Race: Mexico City, 1753," *The Hispanic American Historical Review* 62 (1982): 569–606; and Alicia Tjarks, "Demographic, Ethnic and Occupational Structure of New Mexico in 1790," *The Americas* 35 (1978), 45–88.

There are a number of studies of mission economies. Noteworthy studies include Steven Hackel, "Land, Labor, and Production: The Colonial Economy of Spanish and Mexican California," *California History* LXXVI (Summer–Fall, 1997): 111–146; Cynthia Radding, "The Function of the Market in Changing Economic Structures in the Mission Communities of Pimeria Alta, 1768–1821," *The Americas* 34 (1977): 155–169; "Las estructuras socio-económicas de las misiones de la Pimeria Alta 1768–1850," *Noroeste de Mexico* 3 (1979); and "La acumulación originaria de capital agrario en Sonora," *Noroeste de Mexico* 5 (1981): 15–46. My own contributions appear above. I also want to cite what I consider to be an outstanding study of the indigenous population in the late colonial economy of central Mexico: Arij Ouweneel, *Shadows Over Anáhuac: An Ecological Interpretation of Crisis and Development in Central Mexico, 1730–1810* (Albuquerque, 1996). Ouweneel offers important insights that should inform future studies of economic patterns in northern Mexico.

A number of studies explore the development of mission architecture. A general overview is Rexford Newcomb, *Spanish-Colonial Architecture in the United States* (New York, 1937). For New Mexico see George Kubler, *The Religious Architecture of New Mexico in the Colonial Period and Since the American Occupation* (Colorado Springs, 1940); Joseph Toulouse, "The Mission of San Gregorio de Abo: A Report on the Excavation and Repair of a Seventeenth-Century New Mexico Mission," *Monographs of the School of American Research*, no.13 (Albuquerque, 1949); James E. Ivey, "In the Midst of Loneliness: The Architectural History of the Salinas Missions. Salinas Pueblo Missions National Monument Historic Structure Report," *Southwest Cultural Resources Center Professional Papers,* no.15 (Santa Fe, 1988); and Alden Hayes, *The Four Churches of Pecos* (Albuquerque, 1974). For Sonora and Arizona see Buford Pickens, ed., *The Missions of Northern Sonora: A 1935 Field Documentation* (Tucson, 1933). For the Dominican missions in northern Baja California see Peveril Meigs, *The Dominican Mission Frontier of Lower California* (Berkeley, 1935).

Index

Abo, 29
Acomas, 70
Aguardiente, 19, 20
Aguirre, Manuel, 61
Alta California/Dominicans, building
    construction, 42–46
  adobe style, 42, 44
  churches, 42, 43, 44
  cultural impact, 45–46
  defensive design, 45–46
  map, 38
  Rosario, 42, 43*f*, 44*t*
  Santa Catalina, 45*f*
  Santo Domingo, 43–44
  San Tomás, 44, 46*t*
Alta California/Franciscans
  building construction, 46–55
    churches, 50, 52, 55
    cultural impact, 50, 53
    defensive design, 50
    La Purísima, 47*f*, 48*t*, 50, 51*f*, 52*f*, 53, 54*f*
    Los Berros, 53–55
    map, 38
    Mission Style design, 28
    San Diego, 46
    Santa Clara, 49*f*, 50
  cultural impact
    Chumash, 59, 61, 63
    evangelization, 59, 61, 63
    language barriers, 61
    material culture, 66–67
    religious syncretism, 63
  demographic collapse
    mission resettlement, 93–94, 99–100

Alta California/Franciscans, demographic collapse *(continued)*
    population decline, 108, 109*f*
  economics, labor production, 8–10
    agriculture, 8–9, 18–19
    barley production, 9, 19
    corn production, 9, 19
    craft production, 8–9
    foreign trade, 10
    La Purísima, 9–10
    livestock, 10
    military supply, 9–10, 18–19, 26–27
    overseers, 9
    ranching, 8–9
    wheat production, 9, 19
  economics, local/regional markets, 25–27
  economics, supply system, 18–23
    aguardiente, 19, 20
    Apostolic College (San Fernando), 18
    documentation, 18, 26–27
    foreign trade, 20, 23, 27
    indigenous consumption, 19–20
    military supply, 18–19
    missionary consumption, 19–20
    mission operation, 19–20
    price fluctuations, 20, 21*f*, 22*f*, 23
    wine, 20, 21*f*, 22*f*, 23
  indigenous resistance, 86–87
    corporal punishment, 87
    flight, 87
    La Purísima, 87
    San Diego, 86
    San Gabriel, 86

142   INDEX

Alta California/Franciscans *(continued)*
  mission system
    demise of, 116, 119–24
    legacy of, 127
American Revolutionary War (1775–83), 20
Anza, Juan Bautista de, 6–7
Apaches
  cultural impact, 58, 64
  demographic collapse, 94, 95, 98–99
  indigenous resistance
    New Mexico/Franciscans, 70, 71
    Pimería Alta/Jesuits, 78, 79, 80–83
    Texas/Franciscans, 83–84
Apostolic College, supply system
  Saltillo, 10–11, 12–14, 18
  San Fernando, 18

Baja California/Dominicans
  building construction, 42
    San Francisco de Borja, 39–40
    San Francisco Javier, 35, 40
  indigenous resistance, 74, 75
  mission system legacy, 127
Baja California/Franciscans, building construction, 39
  cultural impact, 40, 42
  map, 36, 37
  San Fernando, 40, 41*f*
  Spanish government involvement, 35
Baja California/Jesuits
  building construction
    churches, 35, 39, 40
    Comondu, 35, 39
    cultural impact, 40, 42
    Loreto, 35
    map, 36, 37
    Mulege, 35
    San Ignacio, 35, 40
    Spanish government involvement, 35
  cultural impact
    evangelization, 57, 58–59, 60, 61–62
    language barriers, 60
    rancherías, 58
    social change, 65–66

Baja California/Jesuits, cultural impact *(continued)*
    traditional beliefs, 65
  demographic collapse
    mission resettlement, 92
    population decline, 107–8
    population estimates, 91–92
  economics, labor production, 8
  indigenous resistance, 71–78
    Cape district, 73, 74–75
    corporal punishment, 72, 76, 77–78
    flight, 74–76, 77
    La Frontera, 71–72
    Loreto, 71
    San Francisco de Borja, 71, 73
    San Ignacio, 71
    San José del Cabo, 73, 74–75
    shamanism, 71, 72–73, 76–77
    Todos Santos, 74–75
  mission system
    demise of, 124
    legacy of, 126–27
Barley, 9, 19
Bourbon Reforms, 18, 24, 35, 42
Building construction
  Abo, 29
  adobe style, 42, 44
  Alta California/Dominicans, 42–46
    adobe style, 42, 44
    churches, 42, 43, 44
    cultural impact, 45–46
    defensive design, 45–46
    map, 38
    Rosario, 42, 43*f*, 44*t*
    Santa Catalina, 45*f*
    Santo Domingo, 43–44
    San Tomás, 44, 46*t*
  Alta California/Franciscans, 46–55
    churches, 50, 52, 55
    cultural impact, 50, 53
    defensive design, 50
    La Purísima, 47*f*, 48*t*, 50, 51*f*, 52*f*, 53, 54*f*
    Los Berros, 53–55
    map, 38
    Mission Style design, 28

INDEX 143

Building construction, Alta California/
Franciscans *(continued)*
San Diego, 46
Santa Clara, 49*f*, 50
architectural style
adobe, 42, 44
Alta California, 42, 44, 45–46, 50
defensive, 29, 33, 35, 45–46, 50
Mission Style, 28
New Mexico/Franciscans, 29, 31
Pimería Alta, 31
Texas/Franciscans, 33, 35
Baja California/Dominicans, 39, 40, 42
San Francisco de Borja, 39–40
San Francisco Javier, 35, 40
Baja California/Franciscans, 35, 39, 40
cultural impact, 40, 42
map, 36, 37
San Fernando, 40, 41*f*
Spanish government involvement, 35
Baja California/Jesuits, 35, 39, 40, 42
churches, 35, 39, 40
Comondu, 35, 39
cultural impact, 40, 42
Loreto, 35
map, 36, 37
Mulege, 35
San Ignacio, 35, 40
Spanish government involvement, 35
churches
Alta California, 42, 43, 44, 50, 52, 55
Baja California, 35, 39, 40
Comondu, 35, 39
contemporary interest, 28, 56
cultural impact
Alta California, 45–46, 50, 53
Baja California, 40, 42
New Mexico/Franciscans, 29, 31
Pimería Alta, 31
Texas/Franciscans, 33, 35
defensive design
Alta California, 45–46, 50

Building construction, defensive design
(continued)
New Mexico/Franciscans, 29
Texas/Franciscans, 33, 35
Giusewa, 29
Humanas, 29
La Purísima, 47*f*, 48*t*, 50, 51*f*, 52*f*, 53, 54*f*
Loreto, 35
Los Berros, 53–55
Mission Style design, 28
Mulege, 35
New Mexico/Franciscans, 29–31
Abo, 29
architectural style, 29, 31
cultural impact, 29, 31
defensive design, 29
Giusewa, 29
Humanas, 29
map, 30
Pecos, 31
Quarai, 29
size, 29, 31
overview, 28–29, 55–56
Pecos, 31
Pimería Alta/Jesuits, 31–32
architectural style, 31
cultural impact, 31
map, 32
Quarai, 29
Rosario, 42, 43*f*, 44*t*
San Diego, 46
San Fernando, 40, 41*f*
San Francisco de Borja, 39–40
San Francisco Javier, 40
San Ignacio, 35, 40
Santa Catalina, 45*f*
Santa Clara, 49*f*, 50
Santo Domingo, 43–44
San Tomás, 44, 46*t*
Spanish government involvement
Baja California, 35
progress reports, 29
Texas/Franciscans, 33–35
architectural style, 33, 35

144 INDEX

Building construction, Texas/Franciscans *(continued)*
    cultural impact, 33, 35
    defensive design, 33, 35
    map, 34

Cape district, 73, 74–75
Caste system, 112–15
    New Mexico/Franciscans, 112
    Pimería Alta/Jesuits, 112, 113–14
    racial identification, 113, 114–15
Cevallos, Juan de, 7–8
Chihuahua trade, 23
Children
    cultural impact, 59–60
    mortality rate, 100
Chumash
    cultural impact, 59, 61, 63
    demographic collapse, 93–94
    language barriers, 61
Chumash revolt (1824), 10, 61
Clavigero, Francisco, 60
Clothing, 63–64, 65–66
Coahuiltecans, 58
Comanches
    cultural impact, 58, 64
    indigenous resistance, 83–84
Comondu, 35, 39
Corn, 6
    California/Franciscans, 9, 19
    Texas/Franciscans, 10
Coronado, Francisco de, 69, 91
Corporal punishment
    demographic collapse, 104
    indigenous resistance
        Alta California/Franciscans, 87
        Baja California/Jesuits, 72, 76, 77–78
    labor production, 5
Crafts, 8–9
Cultural impact
    Alta California/Franciscans
        Chumash, 59, 61, 63
        evangelization, 59, 61, 63
        language barriers, 61
        material culture, 66–67
        religious syncretism, 63

Cultural impact *(continued)*
    Baja California/Jesuits
        evangelization, 57, 58–59, 60, 61–62
        language barriers, 60
        rancherías, 58
        social change, 65–66
        traditional beliefs, 65
    building construction
        Alta California, 45–46, 50, 53
        Baja California, 40, 42
        New Mexico, 29, 31
        Pimería Alta, 31
        Texas, 33, 35
    clothing, 63–64, 65–66
    drug usage, 65
    evangelization, 59–64
        adults, 59
        Alta California/Franciscans, 59, 61, 63
        Baja California/Jesuits, 57, 58–59, 60, 61–62
        baptism, 61–62
        children, 59–60
        communion, 61–62
        language barriers, 60–61
        New Mexico/Franciscans, 57, 62–63
        Pimería Alta/Jesuits, 60–61, 62
        religious syncretism, 62–63
        Spanish government involvement, 59
        Texas/Franciscans, 57–58
        traditional beliefs, 60, 61–63, 65
    infanticide, 65
    language barriers
        Alta California/Franciscans, 61
        Baja California/Jesuits, 60
        Chumash, 61
        Pimería Alta/Jesuits, 60–61
    material culture
        Alta California/Franciscans, 66–67
        La Purísima, 66, 67
        San Antonio, 66, 67
        Soledad, 66–67
    New Mexico/Franciscans
        evangelization, 57, 62–63
        religious syncretism, 62–63
        traditional beliefs, 63

INDEX   145

Cultural impact *(continued)*
Pimería Alta/Jesuits
  drug usage, 65
  evangelization, 60–61, 62
  language barriers, 60–61
  seasonal transhumance, 64
  social change, 64, 65
  traditional beliefs, 65
polygamy, 65
religious syncretism
  Alta California/Franciscans, 63
  New Mexico/Franciscans, 62–63
seasonal transhumance, 64
social change, 63–66
  Baja California/Jesuits, 65–66
  clothing, 63–64, 65–66
  drug usage, 65
  infanticide, 65
  Pimería Alta/Jesuits, 64, 65
  polygamy, 65
  seasonal transhumance, 64
  Texas/Franciscans, 64
Spanish government involvement
  evangelization, 59
  expenditures, 66
Texas/Franciscans
  Apaches, 58, 64
  Coahuiltecans, 58
  Comanches, 58, 64
  evangelization, 57–58
  Hasinais, 57
  Karankawas, 58, 64
  Orcoquisac, 57–58
  seasonal transhumance, 64
  social change, 64
traditional beliefs, 60, 61–63, 65
  Baja California/Jesuits, 65
  New Mexico/Franciscans, 63
  Pimería Alta/Jesuits, 65

Demographic collapse
Alta California/Franciscans
  mission resettlement, 93–94, 99–100
  population decline, 108, 109*f*
Baja California/Jesuits
  mission resettlement, 92

Demographic collapse, Baja California Jesuits *(continued)*
  population decline, 107–8
  population estimates, 91–92
caste system, 112–15
  New Mexico/Franciscans, 112
  Pimería Alta/Jesuits, 112, 113–14
  racial identification, 113, 114–15
causes of, 100, 104–5
  child mortality, 100
  corporal punishment, 104
  disease, 100, 104–5
  medication, 104–5
  social humiliation, 100, 104
mission resettlement, 92–100
  Alta California/Franciscans, 93–94, 99–100
  Apaches, 94, 95, 98–99
  Baja California/Jesuits, 92
  Chumash, 93–94
  food supply, 93–94, 95, 96, 98
  Hasinais, 94
  Karankawas, 94–96, 98
  material goods, 92, 93
  New Mexico/Franciscans, 100, 103*f*
  Pimería Alta/Jesuits, 92–93
  Refugio, 95–96, 98
  Rosario, 95–96, 97*f*, 98
  Texas/Franciscans, 92, 94–100, 101*f*, 102*f*
  water supply, 92, 93
New Mexico/Franciscans
  caste system, 112
  mission resettlement, 100, 103*f*
  population decline, 108, 110–12
  population estimates, 91
overview, 89
Pimería Alta/Jesuits
  caste system, 112, 113–14
  mission resettlement, 92–93
  population decline, 105, 106*f*
population decline, 105–12
  Alta California/Franciscans, 108, 109*f*
  Baja California/Jesuits, 107–8

146 INDEX

Demographic collapse, population decline *(continued)*
  New Mexico/Franciscans, 108, 110–12
  Pimería Alta/Jesuits, 105, 106*f*
  Texas/Franciscans, 105, 107
 population estimates, 89–92
  Baja California/Jesuits, 91–92
  bias in, 89–90
  Karankawas, 91
  migration factor, 90
  mission records, 90
  New Mexico/Franciscans, 91
  Texas/Franciscans, 91
  unit measurements, 90
 Texas/Franciscans
  mission resettlement, 92, 94–100, 101*f*, 102*f*
  population decline, 105, 107
  population estimates, 91
Disease, 100, 104–5
Dominicans. *See specific area/subject*
Drug usage, 65

Economics, labor production, 4–10
 Alta California/Franciscans, 8–10
  agriculture, 8–9, 18–19
  barley production, 9, 19
  corn production, 9, 19
  craft production, 8–9
  foreign trade, 10
  La Purísima, 9–10
  livestock, 10
  military supply, 9–10, 18–19, 26–27
  overseers, 9
  ranching, 8–9
  wheat production, 9, 19
 Baja California/Jesuits, 8
 barley, 9, 19
 corn, 6
  California/Franciscans, 9, 19
  Texas/Franciscans, 10
 corporal punishment, 5
 crafts, 8–9
 encomienda system
  decline of, 5

Economics, labor production, encomienda system *(continued)*
  labor draft, 5
  origins of, 4
  tribute, 4–5
 foreign trade, 10
 indigenous education
  frontier integration, 7
  sociocultural engineering, 4
 La Purísima, 9–10
 livestock, 6
  California/Franciscans, 10
 military supply, 9–10, 18–19, 26–27
 New Mexico/Franciscans, 4
  sociocultural engineering, 4
 objective of, 4
 overseers, 9
 overview, 3
 Pimería Alta/Franciscans
  administration changes, 6–8
  civil administration, 6
  missionary administration, 6–8
  voluntary labor, 6–7
 Pimería Alta/Jesuits
  administration changes, 6
  communal projects, 5
  corporal punishment, 5
  Jesuit expulsion, 6, 26
  wheat production, 6
 ranching
  California/Franciscans, 8–9
  Texas/Franciscans, 10
 Spanish government involvement, 6–7, 8
 Texas/Franciscans, 8
  corn production, 10
  ranching, 10
 wheat, 6
  California/Franciscans, 9, 19
  Pimería Alta/Jesuits, 6
Economics, local/regional markets, 23–27
 Alta California/Franciscans, 25–27
 Chihuahua trade, 23
 foreign trade, 25–26
 La Cieneguilla, 24–25

Economics, local/regional markets *(continued)*
  mining influence, 24–25
  New Mexico/Franciscans, 23
  Pimería Alta/Jesuits
    mining influence, 24–25
    population mobility, 24–25
  Spanish government involvement, 25–26
Economics, supply system, 10–23
  aguardiente, 19, 20
  Alta California/Franciscans, 18–23
    aguardiente, 19, 20
    Apostolic College (San Fernando), 18
    documentation, 18, 26–27
    foreign trade, 20, 23, 27
    indigenous consumption, 19–20
    military supply, 18–19
    missionary consumption, 19–20
    mission operation, 19–20
    price fluctuations, 20, 21*f*, 22*f*, 23
    wine, 20, 21*f*, 22*f*, 23
  Apostolic College
    Saltillo, 10–11, 12–14, 18
    San Fernando, 18
  documentation, 18, 26–27
  flota system, 11–12
  foreign trade, 20, 23, 27
  indigenous consumption
    California/Franciscans, 19–20
    Texas/Franciscans, 11
  military supply, 9–10, 18–19, 26–27
  missionary consumption
    California/Franciscans, 19–20
    Texas/Franciscans, 11, 13, 18
  mission operation
    California/Franciscans, 19–20
    Texas/Franciscans, 11
  price fluctuations
    California/Franciscans, 20, 21*f*, 22*f*, 23
    Texas/Franciscans, 11–12, 14–17*t*, 18
  Spanish government involvement, 11–12, 20
  spices, 11, 12, 18
  Texas/Franciscans, 10–18, 27

Economics, supply system, Texas/Franciscans *(continued)*
  Apostolic College (Saltillo), 10–11, 12–14, 18
  indigenous consumption, 11
  missionary consumption, 11, 13, 18
  mission operation, 11
  price fluctuations, 11–12, 14–17*t*, 18
  spices, 11, 12, 18
  wheat flour, 12–13
  wine, 11, 12
  wheat flour, 12–13
  wine
    California/Franciscans, 20, 21*f*, 22*f*, 23
    Texas/Franciscans, 11, 12
Education, indigenous
  frontier integration, 7
  sociocultural engineering, 4
Encomienda system
  decline of, 5
  labor draft, 5
  origins of, 4
  tribute, 4–5

Flota system, 11–12
Foreign trade
  labor production, 10
  local/regional markets, 25–26
  supply system, 20, 23, 27
Franciscans. *See specific area/subject*
French Revolutionary War, 20

Galvez, José de, 6, 27, 35
Giusewa, 29

Hasinais
  cultural impact, 57
  demographic collapse, 94
  indigenous resistance, 85–86
Hopis, 70–71
Humanas, 29

Independence wars (Mexico) (1810–21), 23, 27, 83

148   INDEX

Infanticide, 65

Jesuits. *See specific area/subject*

Karankawas
  cultural impact, 58, 64
  demographic collapse
    mission resettlement, 94–96, 98
    population estimates, 91
  indigenous resistance, 84–85

La Cieneguilla mining, 24–25
La Frontera, 71–72
Language barriers
  Alta California/Franciscans, 61
  Baja California/Jesuits, 60
  Chumash, 61
  evangelization and, 60–61
  Pimería Alta/Jesuits, 60–61
La Purísima
  building construction, 47*f*, 48*t*, 50, 51*f*, 52*f*, 53, 54*f*
  labor production, 9–10
  material culture, 66, 67
Livestock
  labor production, 6
    California/Franciscans, 10
  mission system demise, 120, 121*f*, 122, 124
Loreto
  building construction, 35
  indigenous resistance, 71
Los Berros, 53–55

Material culture
  Alta California/Franciscans, 66–67
  La Purísima, 66, 67
  San Antonio, 66, 67
  Soledad, 66–67
Medication, 104–5
Migration
  demographic collapse, 90
  seasonal transhumance, 64
Military supply, 9–10, 18–19, 26–27
Mining influence, 24–25

Mission system
  demise of, 116–25
    Alta California/Franciscans, 116, 119–24
    Baja California/Jesuits, 124
    Catholic Church control, 117–18
    demographic collapse, 116, 117, 125
    indigenous emancipation, 119–20
    indigenous integration, 124–25
    land distribution, 120, 122, 123*f*, 124
    livestock distribution, 120, 121*f*, 122, 124
    Mexican government involvement, 118–19
    Mexican liberalism, 117–18, 119
    mission secularization, 116–17, 118, 119–20
    Pimería Alta/Jesuits, 116, 124
    Spaniard expulsion, 118–19
    Spanish government involvement, 116, 117, 118, 124
    Spanish reformers, 116
    Texas/Franciscans, 117, 124
  legacy of, 126–29
    academic glorification, 123
    Alta California/Franciscans, 127
    Baja California/Dominicans, 127
    Baja California/Jesuits, 126–27
    indigenous consciousness, 127–28
    New Mexico/Franciscans, 126
    Pimería Alta/Jesuits, 126
    Serra canonization, 123
    Texas/Franciscans, 126
  overview, xiii-xix
    academic glorification, xiii
    Baja California, xvii
    Catholic Church role, xiv
    central Mexico legacy, xiii-xv
    Chichimec conversion, xvi
    Chichimec War (1550–90), xv-xvi
    convert role models, xvi
    corporal punishment, xv
    demise of, xix
    demographic collapse, xix

Mission system, overview *(continued)*
  Dominicans, xvii
  economics, xviii
  Franciscans, xvi, xvii
  Jesuits, xvi, xvii
  missionary control, xv
  missionary fiefdom, xiv-xv
  missionary time limit, xv
  northern Mexico, xiii, xv-xvii
  resistance to, xviii
  Serra canonization, xiii
  Spanish exploitation, xiii-xiv
Mulege, 35

Napoleonic War, 20
New Mexico/Franciscans
  building construction, 29–31
    Abo, 29
    architectural style, 29, 31
    cultural impact, 29, 31
    defensive design, 29
    Giusewa, 29
    Humanas, 29
    map, 30
    Pecos, 31
    Quarai, 29
    size, 29, 31
  cultural impact
    evangelization, 57, 62–63
    religious syncretism, 62–63
    traditional beliefs, 63
  demographic collapse
    caste system, 112
    mission resettlement, 100, 103*f*
    population decline, 108, 110–12
    population estimates, 91
  economics, labor production, 4
    sociocultural engineering, 4
  economics, local/regional markets, 23
  indigenous resistance, 69–71
    Acomas, 70
    Apaches, 70, 71
    Hopis, 70–71
    Pueblo revolt (1680), 5, 29, 31, 70–71, 88
  mission system legacy, 126

Oñate, Juan de, 4, 69–70
Orcoquisac, 57–58

Payeras, Mariano, 53–54, 55
Pecos, 31
Pimería Alta/Franciscans, labor production
  administration changes, 6–8
  civil administration, 6
  missionary administration, 6–8
  voluntary labor, 6–7
Pimería Alta/Jesuits
  building construction, 31–32
    architectural style, 31
    cultural impact, 31
    map, 32
  cultural impact
    drug usage, 65
    evangelization, 60–61, 62
    language barriers, 60–61
    seasonal transhumance, 64
    social change, 64, 65
    traditional beliefs, 65
  demographic collapse
    caste system, 112, 113–14
    mission resettlement, 92–93
    population decline, 105, 106*f*
  economics, labor production
    administration changes, 6
    communal projects, 5
    corporal punishment, 5
    Jesuit expulsion, 6, 26
    wheat production, 6
  economics, local/regional markets
    mining influence, 24–25
    population mobility, 24–25
  indigenous resistance, 78–83
    Apaches, 78, 79, 80–83
    Pimas, 78–80
    Santa María del Pópulo, 80
    Seris, 78, 79, 80
    Spanish government involvement, 82–83
  mission system
    demise of, 116, 124
    legacy of, 126
Polygamy, 65

150 INDEX

Population. *See* Demographic collapse
Price fluctuations, supply system
   California/Franciscans, 20, 21*f*, 22*f*, 23
   Texas/Franciscans, 11–12, 14–17*t*, 18
Pueblo revolt (1680), 5, 29, 31, 70–71, 88

Quarai, 29

Ranching
   California/Franciscans, 8–9
   Texas/Franciscans, 10
Religious syncretism
   Alta California/Franciscans, 63
   New Mexico/Franciscans, 62–63
Resistance, indigenous
   Alta California/Franciscans, 86–87
      corporal punishment, 87
      flight, 87
      La Purísma, 87
      San Diego, 86
      San Gabriel, 86
   Baja California/Dominicans, 74, 75
   Baja California/Jesuits, 71–78
      Cape district, 73, 74–75
      corporal punishment, 72, 76, 77–78
      flight, 74–76, 77
      La Frontera, 71–72
      Loreto, 71
      San Francisco de Borja, 71, 73
      San Ignacio, 71
      San José del Cabo, 73, 74–75
      shamanism, 71, 72–73, 76–77
      Todos Santos, 74–75
   corporal punishment
      Alta California/Franciscans, 87
      Baja California/Jesuits, 72, 76, 77–78
   flight
      Alta California/Franciscans, 87
      Baja California/Jesuits, 74–76, 77
   New Mexico/Franciscans, 69–71
      Acomas, 70
      Apaches, 70, 71
      Hopis, 70–71
      Pueblo revolt (1680), 5, 29, 31, 70–71, 88
      overview, 68–69, 88

Resistance, indigenous *(continued)*
   Pimería Alta/Jesuits, 78–83
      Apaches, 78, 79, 80–83
      Pimas, 78–80
      Santa María del Pópulo, 80
      Seris, 78, 79, 80
      Spanish government involvement, 82–83
   shamanism, 71, 72–73, 76–77
   Spanish government involvement, 82–83
      Texas/Franciscans, 83–84, 85–86
   Texas/Franciscans, 83–86
      Apaches, 83–84
      Comanches, 83–84
      Hasinais, 85–86
      Karankawas, 84–85
      Spanish government involvement, 83–84, 85–86
Rosario
   building construction, 42, 43*f*, 44*t*
   demographic collapse, 95–96, 97*f*, 98

San Antonio, 66, 67
San Diego
   building construction, 46
   indigenous resistance, 86
San Fernando, 40, 41*f*
San Francisco de Borja
   building construction, 39–40
   indigenous resistance, 71, 73
San Francisco Javier, 35, 40
San Gabriel, 86
San Ignacio
   building construction, 35, 40
   indigenous resistance, 71
San José del Cabo, 73, 74–75
Santa Catalina, 45*f*
Santa Clara, 49*f*, 50
Santa María del Pópulo, 80
Santo Domingo, 43–44
San Tomás, 44, 46*t*
Seasonal transhumance, 64
Secularization, 116–17, 118, 119–20
Serra, Junipero, xiii, 123
Seven Years' War (1756–63), 11, 18, 86

INDEX   151

Shamanism, 71, 72–73, 76–77
Soledad, 66–67
Sonora. *See* Pimería Alta/Franciscans;
    Pimería Alta/Jesuits
Spanish government involvement
  building construction
    Baja California, 35
    progress reports, 29
  cultural impact
    evangelization, 59
    expenditures, 66
  economics
    labor production, 6–7, 8
    local/regional markets, 25–26
    supply system, 11–12, 20
  indigenous resistance, 82–83
  mission system demise, 116, 117, 118, 124
Spices, 11, 12, 18

Texas/Franciscans
  building construction, 33–35
    architectural style, 33, 35
    cultural impact, 33, 35
    defensive design, 33, 35
    map, 34
  cultural impact
    Apaches, 58, 64
    Coahuiltecans, 58
    Comanches, 58, 64
    evangelization, 57–58
    Hasinais, 57
    Karankawas, 58, 64
    Orcoquisac, 57–58
    seasonal transhumance, 64
    social change, 64
  demographic collapse
    mission resettlement, 92, 94–100, 101*f*, 102*f*
    population decline, 105, 107
    population estimates, 91
  economics, labor production, 8
    corn production, 10
    ranching, 10
  economics, supply system, 10–18, 27

Texas/Franciscans, *(continued)*
  Apostolic College (Saltillo), 10–11, 12–14, 18
  indigenous consumption, 11
  missionary consumption, 11, 13, 18
  mission operation, 11
  price fluctuations, 11–12, 14–17*t*, 18
  spices, 11, 12, 18
  wheat flour, 12–13
  wine, 11, 12
  indigenous resistance, 83–86
    Apaches, 83–84
    Comanches, 83–84
    Hasinais, 85–86
    Karankawas, 84–85
    Spanish government involvement, 83–84, 85–86
  mission system
    demise of, 117, 124
    legacy of, 126
Todos Santos, 74–75
Traditional beliefs
  Baja California/Jesuits, 65
  evangelization and, 60, 61–63, 65
  indigenous resistance, 71, 72–73, 76–77
  New Mexico/Franciscans, 63
  Pimería Alta/Jesuits, 65
  shamanism, 71, 72–73, 76–77

Vargas, Diego de, 5, 70

War of Austrian Succession (1742–48), 11, 18
Wheat
  labor production, 6
  California/Franciscans, 9, 19
  Pimería Alta/Jesuits, 6
  supply system, 12–13
Wine
  California/Franciscans, 20, 21*f*, 22*f*, 23
  Texas/Franciscans, 11, 12

Ximeno, Diego, 7

About the Author

Robert Jackson received his doctorate in 1988 from the University of California, Berkeley, with a specialization in Latin American history. He has authored or edited eight books and over forty journal articles. His latest book, *Race, Caste, and Status: Indians in Colonial Spanish America* (1999) was cited as an outstanding academic book for 1999 by *Choice* magazine. He currently teaches at SUNY College at Oneonta, New York.

For Product Safety Concerns and Information please contact our EU representative GPSR@taylorandfrancis.com
Taylor & Francis Verlag GmbH, Kaufingerstraße 24, 80331 München, Germany